Mediterranean DIET Cookbook

FULL-COLOR EDITION

1800+ Days
of Amazing Mouthwatering Healthy Recipes
Build Healthy Habits, Living and Eating
Well Every Day

Isabella Williams

© Copyright 2023 by Isabella Williams - All rights reserved.

All rights reserved. No part of this book may be reproduced in any form without permission in writing from the author. Reviewers may quote brief passages in reviews.

While all attempts have been made to verify the information provided in this publication, neither the author nor the publisher assumes any responsibility for errors, omissions, or contrary interpretations of the subject matter herein. The views expressed in this publication are those of the author and should not be taken as expert instruction or commands. The reader is responsible for their actions and their interpretation of the material found within this publication.

Adherence to all applicable laws and regulations, including international, federal, state, and local governing professional licensing, business practices, advertising, and all other aspects of doing business in the US, Canada, or any other jurisdiction, is the sole responsibility of the reader and consumer.

Neither the author nor the publisher assumes any responsibility or liability whatsoever on behalf of the consumer or reader of this material. Any perceived slight of any individual or organization is purely unintentional.

Table of Contents

Introduction 5

Chapter 1.
Fundamentals Of the Mediterranean Diet 6

Chapter 2.
The Mediterranean Diet Pyramid 8

Chapter 3.
Foods to Eat and to Avoid 10

Chapter 4.
Breaking Down the Health Benefits 12

Chapter 5.
Breakfast recipes 14

Chapter 6.
Lunch recipes 25

Chapter 7.
Dinner recipes 34

Chapter 8.
Snack ideas 43

Chapter 9.
Sweet desserts 49

Chapter 10.
30-Day meal plan 57

Chapter 11.
Cooking conversion chart 60

Conclusion 63

Recipe Index 65

Introduction

Following a Mediterranean diet has been linked to numerous health benefits, including a reduced risk of heart disease and stroke. This eating plan prioritizes whole foods such as fruits, vegetables, lean proteins, and whole grains while limiting highly processed, sugary, and fatty foods. Along with a balanced diet, habits such as regular physical activity and stress management are key components of a healthier life. Furthermore, adopting a Mediterranean diet can be pleasurable, as it emphasizes flavorful herbs and spices, nutritious fats, and fresh produce.

In addition to the health benefits, following a Mediterranean diet has also been associated with a longer lifespan and a lower risk of cognitive decline in older adults. Studies have shown that this diet is rich in antioxidants and anti-inflammatory compounds, which could improve overall brain health. Additionally, the Mediterranean lifestyle emphasizes social connection and mindfulness during meals, which can positively impact mental and emotional well-being. This dietary pattern offers a holistic approach to improving health and quality of life by prioritizing wholesome, nourishing foods and overall wellness.

In this cookbook, you will discover a wide variety of delicious and nutritious dishes that follow the principles of the Mediterranean diet. From fresh seafood to hearty grains, each recipe has been thoughtfully crafted to incorporate the abundant flavors and ingredients of the region. A detailed nutritional breakdown accompanies each recipe to enable easy tracking of daily nutrient requirements. Along with the recipes, readers will gain insight into the cultural significance, health benefits, and cooking principles underlying the Mediterranean diet.

Eating like in the Mediterranean has never been easier, with various recipes provided to suit every taste and occasion. By incorporating these wholesome dishes into your daily routine, you can improve your overall health and well-being while indulging in the Mediterranean region's cultural richness.

CHAPTER 1
Fundamentals Of the Mediterranean Diet

The Mediterranean diet is a way of eating enjoyed for centuries - dating back to the Greek and Roman empires. It is a heart-healthy way of eating based on the traditional foods and cooking styles of countries bordering the Mediterranean Sea. With its emphasis on fresh fruits and vegetables, whole grains, legumes, seafood, and olive oil, this way of eating has been credited with helping people to live longer, healthier lives. The Mediterranean lifestyle also includes moderate exercise and encourages social activity, providing many health benefits that continue to be studied and evaluated today. While the diet has always been popular in the region, its benefits have recently gained international recognition, leading to increased adoption worldwide.

Its consumption has been associated with lower risks of heart-related ailments, type-2 diabetes, cognitive decline, and several types of cancer. Further studies have also suggested that the diet could be an effective weight-loss strategy. Additionally, the Mediterranean lifestyle has been found to impact mental health positively - the combination of healthy food choices, regular physical activities, and social activities seems to promote better emotional and cognitive health. With such a wide range of health benefits, it is no surprise that the Mediterranean diet continues gaining popularity and inspiring people to embrace its nutrient-rich culinary culture.

Beyond this, the diet's reputation for being delicious and varied has not only made it a go-to for those looking to improve their health but has pushed it to the forefront of modern cuisine, inspiring chefs to infuse flavors into a variety of dishes that historically date back to the diet's rich culture. Many restaurants and home cooks alike have also incorporated the Mediterranean diet into their menus or meal planning. By using simple yet high-quality ingredients, they can easily create mouthwatering dishes that are both healthy and flavorful. Recipes for classic Mediterranean dishes like Greek salad, tabbouleh, vegetable stew, and fish fillet have become mainstays in modern cuisine, contributing to the diet's expanding popularity. With such a vast range of culinary choices and an overall focus on well-being, it's no wonder that the Mediterranean diet remains a top choice for those seeking both delicious and healthy meals. With time, a conscious effort, and dedication, you can make gradual changes and create delicious meals that will make this diet enjoyable for years to come. So, make every meal count and savor the flavors of the Mediterranean diet with every bite.

Fundamentals of the mediterranean diet

CHAPTER 2
The Mediterranean Diet Pyramid

The Mediterranean Diet Pyramid is an excellent way to understand the types of foods and portions that should be included in a nutritious Mediterranean diet. The pyramid consists of the following:

1. The pyramid's base consists of the daily consumption of fruits, vegetables, legumes, grains, herbs, spices, seeds, and nuts. Fruits and vegetables should be the focus of the diet, making up the majority of the calories consumed each day. Legumes, such as beans, lentils, and peas, are also a large part of the diet and can be incorporated into many dishes. Whole grains, such as wheat and oats, are also included in the pyramid, as well as nuts, which can be a great source of healthy fats, such as omega-3 fatty acids. Herbs and spices can also be used for flavoring and can help to reduce the amount of added salt needed when cooking. Additionally, olive oil should be the fat of choice, as it is a great source of healthy fat and is a staple in the Mediterranean Diet.

2. The next level of the Mediterranean Diet Pyramid is comprised of fish and seafood that should be consumed at least twice a week. This could include salmon, cod, sardines, herring, mackerel, and other types of fish. Oily fish, such as salmon, contain important omega-3 fats, which are beneficial for brain function and cardiovascular health. Seafood, such as shrimp and prawns, are also beneficial sources of lean protein and essential vitamins and minerals.

3. The third level of the pyramid includes smaller amounts of cheese, yogurt, and eggs, which should be consumed in moderation. Dairy is an important part of a balanced diet and provides essential nutrients, such as calcium and vitamin D, as well as protein. Eggs are also great sources of pro-

tein, vitamins, and minerals. It's important to note that dairy and eggs are only recommended in moderation, as they can be higher in saturated fats.

4. The top of the pyramid includes red meat and sweets, which should be consumed in moderation. Red meat is an important source of protein, iron, and other essential vitamins and minerals. However, it is also high in saturated fats, so it's best to limit one's intake of red meat and opt for leaner cuts when possible. Sweets should also be consumed in moderation, as they contain empty calories and are high in sugar.

The Mediterranean diet is not just about consuming certain foods but also about the lifestyle it encourages. It also emphasizes physical activity and social interaction, which can benefit one's health. Regular physical activity is important for managing weight and overall health and can help to reduce the risk of chronic diseases. Socializing and spending time with friends and family are also associated with improved overall well-being. Overall, the Mediterranean Diet Pyramid is a great way to understand what a nutritious Mediterranean diet looks like and how to balance all the components for optimal health.

The mediterranean diet pyramid

CHAPTER 3
Foods to Eat & to Avoid

The Mediterranean Diet varies depending upon the source you take it from; however, it has some basic principles. Let's look at the do-eats and don't eat when following this healthy lifestyle.

Do eat:

- Fresh vegetables
- Olives
- Fresh fruits
- Nuts, such as almonds, walnuts, macadamia nuts, and hazelnuts, in particular
- Seeds, such as sunflower and pumpkin seeds
- Potatoes, including sweet potatoes
- Legumes, e.g., peas, beans, lentils, pulses, chickpeas, peanuts
- Wholegrains, such as whole oats, barley, brown rice, whole grain pasta
- Bread, as long as it is wholegrain/brown bread
- Herbs
- Fresh fish, such as sardines, salmon, tuna, mackerel, trout, mussels, crab, and shrimp, in particular
- Seafood
- Spices
- Olive oil, particularly the extra virgin variety
- Avocados and avocado oil
- Plenty of water
- 1 glass of red wine per day
- Coffee and tea, as long as you don't sweeten them

You can also eat the following with a few restrictions:

- Eggs – in moderation
- Cheese – in moderation
- Yogurt (including Greek yogurt) – in moderation
- Chicken and other poultry products – in moderation

> Red meat – occasionally

You should avoid eating:

> Processed meat products, such as hot dogs or packaged burgers, etc.
> Other foods are processed, such as low-fat foods or anything which is labeled as 'diet.'
> Refined oils, such as canola oil, soybean oil, etc.
> Refined grains, such as white bread
> Trans fats, including margarine
> Anything which contains added sugars, such as ice cream, candies, etc.

Beverages that are sweetened with sugar, such as cola

As you can see, the Mediterranean Diet encourages the consumption of whole and minimally processed foods that are naturally rich and operate in cohesion to boost one's health. Incorporating these into your eating habits may provide your body with the energy and nutrient requirements it needs without encouraging excessive weight gain or the development of other chronic diseases.

CHAPTER 4
Breaking Down the Health Benefits

The Mediterranean diet is considered the healthiest as it is primarily based on the traditional foods and flavors of the countries surrounding the Mediterranean Sea. Numerous studies have shown that following this diet can lead to a variety of health benefits, such as:

1. **Improved cardiovascular health** - Following the Mediterranean diet has been linked to better cardiovascular health, with studies demonstrating a reduced risk for heart disease, stroke, and heart attack. This may be due to the diet's emphasis on fresh produce, lean protein, healthy fats, and a lower intake of processed and sugary foods. The diet is also rich in antioxidants and anti-inflammatory compounds, which can benefit heart health by reducing inflammation and oxidative stress in the body.

2. **Reduced risk of chronic diseases** - Studies have found that people who follow a Mediterranean diet have a reduced risk of chronic diseases like type 2 diabetes, Alzheimer's, and certain types of cancer. This diet is typically high in antioxidants, fiber, and healthy fats, which can help protect against the development of these diseases.

3. **Healthier weight management** - The Mediterranean diet has been shown to aid in weight management. The diet emphasizes whole and nutrient-dense foods over processed alternatives, leading to natural calorie restriction. Additionally, the diet's high fiber and protein content can increase feelings of fullness, further preventing overeating. Due to these factors, following a Mediterranean diet may be a practical and sustainable approach to achieving and maintaining a healthy weight.

4. **Improved cognitive function** - The benefits of the Mediterranean diet extend beyond physical health as it can improve cognitive function. Studies show that following this diet has been linked to reduced cognitive decline and a lower risk of developing conditions such as Alzheimer's disease. The anti-inflammatory compounds in foods such as fish, nuts, and olive oil benefit brain health by reducing oxidation and inflammation. Additionally, a diet rich in antioxidants and diverse nutrients from fruits, vegetables, and whole grains promotes overall brain function. It is a better subject for lifestyle diseases such as depression, bipolar, and anxiety.

5. **A longer and healthier life expectancy** - The Mediterranean diet may also lead to a longer and healthier life expectancy. Research suggests that individuals who follow this diet may have an increased lifespan and a lower risk of developing age-related diseases. The diet's focus on plant-based foods, healthy fats, and reduced processed foods may contribute to these outcomes. Moreover, the Mediterranean lifestyle encourages moderate physical activity and low to moderate alcohol intake, making it a viable solution for overall wellness.

Ultimately, the Mediterranean diet provides a sustainable and flexible approach to healthy eating that can benefit individuals in many ways. In addition to its numerous health benefits, there is strong evidence of cultural and social connections related to slower eating that improve well-being. Incorporating aspects of the Mediterranean diet into our lifestyles can extend beyond just the food we eat into socializing healthfully. The accumulated research on this pattern is beyond reproach and supports the continuous implements of healthy changes in our everyday routine.

Breaking down the health benefits

CHAPTER 5
BREAKFAST RECIPES

Greek Egg and Tomato Scramble

1 minutes

15-20 minutes

4

Ingredients:

> ¼ cup extra-virgin olive oil, divided
> 1½ cups chopped fresh tomatoes
> ¼ cup finely minced red onion
> 2 garlic cloves, minced
> ½ tsp dried oregano
> ½ tsp dried thyme
> 8 large eggs
> ½ tsp salt
> ¼ tsp freshly ground black pepper
> ¾ cup crumbled feta cheese
> ¼ cup chopped fresh mint leaves

Directions:

1. In your large skillet, heat the olive oil over medium heat. Add the chopped tomatoes and red onion.
2. Sauté for 10 to 12 minutes until tomatoes are cooked through and soft.
3. Add the garlic, oregano, and thyme and sauté for 2 to 4 minutes, until fragrant and the liquid has reduced.
4. Whisk together the eggs, salt, and pepper in your medium bowl until well combined.
5. Add the eggs to the skillet, reduce the heat to low, and scramble for 3 to 4 minutes until set and creamy.
6. Remove the skillet, stir in the feta and mint, and serve warm.

Nutrition: Calories: 338; Fat: 28g; Carbs: 6g; Protein: 16g

Fig and Ricotta Toast

Ingredients:

> ¼ cup ricotta cheese
> 2 pieces whole-wheat bread, toasted
> 4 figs, halved
> 2 tbsp walnuts, chopped
> 1 tsp honey

Directions:

1. Spread 2 tablespoons of ricotta cheese on each piece of toast. Add 4 fig halves to each piece of toast, pressing firmly to keep the figs in the ricotta.
2. Sprinkle 1 tablespoon of walnuts and drizzle ½ teaspoon of honey on each piece of toast.

2

5 minutes

0 minutes

Nutrition: Calories: 215; Fat: 10g; Carbs: 26g; Protein: 7g

Breakfast recipes 15

Poached Eggs with Avocado Purée

10 minutes

5 minutes

4

Ingredients:
> 2 avocados, peeled & pitted
> ¼ cup chopped fresh basil leaves
> 3 tbsp red wine vinegar divided
> Juice of 1 lemon
> Zest of 1 lemon
> 1 garlic clove, minced
> 1 tsp sea salt divided
> ⅛ tsp freshly ground black pepper
> Pinch cayenne pepper, + more as needed
> 4 eggs

Directions:
1. Combine the avocados, basil, 2 tablespoons of vinegar, lemon juice, zest, garlic, ½ tsp sea salt, pepper, and cayenne in a blender. Purée for about 1 minute until smooth.
2. Fill a 12-inch nonstick skillet about three-fourths full of water and place it over medium heat.
3. Add the remaining vinegar and sea salt. Let the water simmer.
4. Carefully crack the eggs into custard cups. Holding the cups just barely above the water, carefully slip the eggs into the simmering water, one at a time.
5. Turn off the heat and cover the skillet. Let the eggs sit for 5 minutes without agitating the pan or removing the lid.
6. Using a slotted spoon, carefully lift the eggs from the water, allowing them to drain completely.
7. Place each egg on a plate and spoon the avocado purée over the top.

Nutrition: Calories: 213; Fat: 20g; Carbs: 11g; Protein: 2g

Breakfast Polenta

Ingredients:
> 2 (18-oz) tubes of plain polenta
> 2¼ to 2½ cups 2% milk, divided
> 2 oranges, peeled & chopped
> ½ cup chopped pecans
> ¼ cup 2% plain Greek yogurt
> 8 tsp honey

Directions:
1. Slice the polenta into rounds and place in a microwave-safe bowl. Heat in the microwave on high for 45 seconds.
2. Transfer the polenta to a large pot, and mash it with a potato masher or fork until coarsely mashed. Place the pot on your stove over medium heat.
3. Heat the milk in your microwave on high for 1 minute in a medium, microwave-safe bowl.
4. Pour 2 cups of the warmed milk into the pot with the polenta, and stir with a whisk.
5. Keep on stirring for 5 minutes and mash with the whisk, adding the remaining milk a few tablespoons at a time until the polenta is fairly smooth. Remove from the stove.
6. Divide the polenta among four serving bowls. Top each bowl with one-quarter of the oranges, 2 tbsp pecans, 1 tbsp yogurt, and 2 tsp honey before serving.

6

5 minutes

10 minutes

Nutrition: Calories: 234; Fat: 7g; Carbs: 38g; Protein: 3g

Asparagus And Swiss Quiche

Ingredients:
- 6 cups water
- 8 oz asparagus, ends trimmed, cut into 1-inch pieces
- 2 tbsp olive oil
- 4 scallions, white and green parts, chopped
- 1 (8-inch) store-bought unbaked pie shell
- 2 large eggs
- ½ cup heavy cream
- 2 tbsp chopped fresh tarragon
- ¼ tsp ground nutmeg
- 1 cup shredded Swiss cheese

Directions:
1. Preheat the oven to 400°F.
2. Bring the water to a boil in your medium pot over medium-high heat. Add the asparagus and blanch within 2 minutes. Drain and set aside.
3. In a skillet over medium heat, heat the olive oil. Add the scallions and cook for 5 minutes. Add the asparagus and cook for 1 minute.
4. Spoon the vegetables into the unbaked pie shell. Set aside.
5. In a medium bowl, whisk the eggs. Add the heavy cream, tarragon, and nutmeg. Whisk to combine well.
6. Pour the egg mixture over the asparagus. Sprinkle the Swiss cheese over the top.
7. Bake for about 40 minutes until firm. Remove from the oven, cool to room temperature, and serve.

20 minutes
43 minutes
6

Nutrition: Calories: 319; Fat: 26g; Carbs: 15g; Protein: 9g

Pomegranate Cherry Smoothie Bowl

Ingredients:
- 1 (16-oz) bag of delicious dark cherries in ice
- 1½ cups of Greek yogurt, 2%
- ¾ cup of juice pomegranate
- cup 2% milk
- 1 tsp vanilla extract
- ¾ tsp ground cinnamon
- 6 ice cubes
- ½ cup chopped pistachios
- ½ cup raw seeds from a pomegranate

Directions:
1. In a blender, combine the cherries, yogurt, milk, vanilla, cinnamon, and ice cubes. Purée until well-combined and fluid.
2. Four bowls will be filled with the smoothie. Serve each immediately after adding 2 teaspoons of pistachios and 2 tablespoons of pomegranate seeds to each.

4
5 minutes
0 minutes

Nutrition: Calories: 212; Fat: 7g; Carbs: 35g; Protein: 4g

Breakfast recipes   17

Greek Yogurt Parfait

5 minutes

0 minutes

1

Ingredients:
> ½ cup plain whole-milk Greek yogurt
> 2 tbsp heavy whipping cream
> ¼ cup frozen berries, thawed with juices
> ½ tsp vanilla or almond extract (optional)
> ¼ tsp ground cinnamon (optional)
> 1 tbsp ground flaxseed
> 2 tbsp chopped nuts (walnuts or pecans)

Directions:
1. In a small bowl or glass, combine the yogurt, heavy whipping cream, thawed berries in their juice, vanilla or almond extract (if using), cinnamon (if using), and flaxseed, and stir well until smooth. Top with chopped nuts, and enjoy.

Nutrition: Calories: 267; Fat: 19g; Carbs: 12g; Protein: 12g

Marinara Eggs with Parsley

Ingredients:
> 1 tbsp extra-virgin olive oil
> 1 cup chopped onion
> 2 garlic cloves, minced
> 2 (14.5-oz) cans Italian diced tomatoes, undrained, no salt added
> 6 large eggs
> ½ cup chopped fresh flat-leaf (Italian) parsley
> Crusty Italian bread and grated Parmesan or Romano cheese for serving (optional)

Directions:
1. In your large skillet over medium-high heat, heat the oil. Add the onion and cook within 5 minutes, stirring often. Add the garlic and cook within 1 minute.
2. Pour the tomatoes with their juices over the onion mixture and cook for 2 to 3 minutes until bubbling.
3. While waiting for the tomato mixture to bubble, crack one egg into a small custard cup or coffee mug.
4. When the tomato mixture bubbles, adjust to medium heat. Then use a large spoon to make six indentations in the tomato mixture.
5. Gently pour the first cracked egg into one indentation and repeat, cracking the remaining eggs, one at a time, into the custard cup and pouring one into each indentation.
6. Cover the skillet and cook for 6 to 7 minutes or until the eggs are done to your liking.
7. Top with the parsley, and serve with the bread and grated cheese, if desired.

6

5 minutes

14-16 minutes

Nutrition: Calories: 122; Fat: 7g; Carbs: 7g; Protein: 7g

Chapter 5

Berry Baked Oatmeal

10 minutes

45-50 minutes

8

Ingredients:
> 2 cups rolled oats
> 2 cups (10-oz bag) of frozen mixed berries
> 2 cups plain, unsweetened almond milk
> 1 cup plain Greek yogurt
> ¼ cup maple syrup
> 2 tbsp extra-virgin olive oil
> 2 tsp ground cinnamon
> 1 tsp baking powder
> 1 tsp vanilla extract
> ½ tsp kosher salt
> ¼ tsp ground nutmeg
> ⅛ tsp ground cloves

Directions:
1. Preheat the oven to 375°F.
2. Mix all the ingredients in your large bowl. Pour into a 9-by-13-inch baking dish. Bake for 45 to 50 minutes or until golden brown.

Nutrition: Calories: 180; Fat: 6g; Carbs: 28g; Protein: 6g

Fruit Bulgur Breakfast Bowl

Ingredients:
> 1½ cups uncooked bulgur
> 2 cups 2% milk
> 1 cup water
> ½ teaspoon ground cinnamon
> 2 cups frozen (or fresh, pitted) dark sweet cherries
> 8 dried (or fresh) figs, chopped
> ½ cup chopped almonds
> ¼ cup loosely packed fresh mint, chopped
> Warm 2% milk for serving (optional)

Directions:
1. Combine the bulgur, milk, water, and cinnamon in a medium saucepan. Stir once, then let it boil.
2. Cover, adjust to medium-low heat, and simmer for 10 minutes or until the liquid is absorbed.
3. Turn off the heat, but keep the pan on the stove, and stir in the frozen cherries (no need to thaw), figs, and almonds.
4. Stir well, cover for 1 minute, let the hot bulgur thaw the cherries, and partially hydrate the figs. Stir in the mint.
5. Scoop into serving bowls. Serve with warm milk, if desired.

6

5 minutes

11 minutes

Nutrition: Calories: 301; Fat: 6g; Carbs: 57g; Protein: 9g

Breakfast recipes

Chocolate Banana Smoothie

Ingredients:
> 2 bananas, peeled
> 1 cup unsweetened almond milk
> 1 cup crushed ice
> 3 tbsp unsweetened cocoa powder
> 3 tbsp honey

Directions:
1. Combine the bananas, almond milk, ice, cocoa powder, and honey in a blender. Blend until smooth. Serve.

5 minutes

0 minutes

2

Nutrition: Calories: 219; Fat: 2g; Carbs: 57g; Protein: 2g

Tomato Avocado Toast

Ingredients:
> 2 tbsp ground flaxseed
> ½ tsp baking powder
> 2 large eggs
> 1 tsp salt, plus more for serving
> ½ tsp freshly ground black pepper, + more for serving
> ½ tsp garlic powder (optional)
> 3 tbsp extra-virgin olive oil, divided
> 1 medium ripe avocado, peeled, pitted, & sliced
> 2 tbsp chopped ripe tomato or salsa

Directions:
1. In a small bowl, combine the flaxseed and baking powder, breaking up any lumps in the baking powder.
2. Add the eggs, salt, pepper, and garlic powder (if using) and whisk well. Let sit for 2 minutes.
3. Heat 1 tablespoon olive oil over medium heat in a small nonstick skillet.
4. Pour the egg mixture into your skillet and cook undisturbed for 2 to 3 minutes until the egg begins to set on the bottom.
5. Using your rubber spatula, scrape down the sides to allow the uncooked egg to reach the bottom. Cook for another 2 to 3 minutes.
6. Once almost set, flip like a pancake and allow the top to cook fully for another 1 to 2 minutes.
7. Remove from the pan and allow to cool slightly. Slice into 2 pieces.
8. Top each "toast" with avocado slices, additional salt, pepper, and chopped tomato, and drizzle with the remaining olive oil.

2

5 minutes

5-8 minutes

Nutrition: Calories: 287; Fat: 25g; Carbs: 3g; Protein: 9g

Harissa Shakshuka with Bell Peppers

10 minutes

23-26 minutes

4

Ingredients:
- 1½ tbsp extra-virgin olive oil
- 2 tbsp harissa
- 1 tbsp tomato paste
- ½ onion, diced
- 1 bell pepper, seeded and diced
- 3 garlic cloves, minced
- 1 (28-oz) can of no-salt-added diced tomatoes
- ½ tsp kosher salt
- 4 large eggs
- 2 to 3 tbsp fresh basil, chopped or cut into ribbons

Directions:
1. Preheat the oven to 375°F.
2. Heat the olive oil in a 12-inch cast-iron pan or ovenproof skillet over medium heat. Add the harissa, tomato paste, onion, and bell pepper.
3. Sauté for 3 to 4 minutes. Add the garlic and cook within 30 seconds until fragrant. Add the diced tomatoes and salt and simmer for 10 minutes.
4. Make 4 wells in the sauce and gently break 1 egg into each. Transfer to your oven and bake for 10 to 12 minutes until the whites are cooked.
5. Allow to cool for 3 to 5 minutes, garnish with the basil, and carefully spoon onto plates.

Nutrition: Calories: 190; Fat: 10g; Carbs: 15g; Protein: 9g

Egg Baked in Avocado

Ingredients:
- 1 large ripe avocado
- 2 large eggs
- Salt & ground black pepper to taste
- 4 tbsp jarred pesto for serving
- 2 tbsp chopped tomato, for serving
- 2 tbsp crumbled feta for serving (optional)

Directions:
1. Preheat the oven to 425°F.
2. Slice your avocado in half and remove the pit. Scoop out about 1 to 2 tablespoons from each half to create a hole large enough to fit an egg.
3. Place the avocado halves on your baking sheet, cut-side up. Crack 1 egg in each avocado half and season with salt and pepper.
4. Bake for 10 to 15 minutes until the eggs are set and cooked to the desired level of doneness.
5. Remove from oven and top each avocado with 2 tablespoons pesto, 1 tablespoon chopped tomato, and 1 tablespoon crumbled feta (if using).

2

5 minutes

10-15 minutes

Nutrition: Calories: 302; Fat: 26g; Carbs: 10g; Protein: 8g

Breakfast recipes 21

Quinoa Breakfast Bowl

10 minutes

10-12 minutes

4

Ingredients:
> 1½ cups water
> 1 cup quinoa
> 2 cinnamon sticks
> 1-inch knob of ginger, peeled
> ¼ tsp kosher salt
> 1 cup plain Greek yogurt
> ½ cup dates, pitted and chopped
> ½ cup almonds (raw or roasted), chopped
> 2 tsp honey (optional)

Directions:
1. Bring the water, quinoa, cinnamon sticks, ginger, and salt to a boil in your medium saucepan over high heat.
2. Adjust to a simmer and cover for 10 to 12 minutes. Remove the cinnamon sticks and ginger—fluff with a fork.
3. Add the yogurt, dates, and almonds to the quinoa and mix them together. Divide evenly among 4 bowls and garnish with ½ tsp honey per bowl, if desired.

Nutrition: Calories: 280; Fat: 11g; Carbs: 37g; Protein: 13g

Tomato and Zucchini Frittata

4

10 minutes

16-18 minutes

Ingredients:
> 3 eggs
> 3 egg whites
> ½ cup unsweetened almond milk
> ½ tsp sea salt
> ⅛ tsp freshly ground black pepper
> 2 tbsp extra-virgin olive oil
> 1 zucchini, chopped
> 8 cherry tomatoes, halved
> ¼ cup (about 2 oz) grated Parmesan cheese

Directions:
1. Heat the oven's broiler to high, adjusting the oven rack to the center position.
2. Whisk the eggs, egg whites, almond milk, sea salt, and pepper in a small bowl. Set aside.
3. Heat the olive oil in your 12-inch ovenproof skillet over medium-high heat until it shimmers.
4. Add the zucchini and tomatoes and cook for 5 minutes, stirring occasionally.
5. Pour the egg mixture over your vegetables and cook for about 4 minutes without stirring until the eggs set around the edges.
6. Using a silicone spatula, pull the set of eggs away from the edges of the pan.
7. Tilt the pan in all directions to allow the unset eggs to fill the spaces along the edges.
8. Continue to cook for about 4 minutes more without stirring until the edges set again.
9. Sprinkle the eggs with the Parmesan. Transfer the pan to the broiler.
10. Cook within 3 to 5 minutes until the cheese melts and the eggs are puffy. Cut into wedges to serve.

Nutrition: Calories: 223; Fat: 4g; Carbs: 13g; Protein: 14g

Honey Nut Granola

10 minutes

22 minutes

6

Ingredients:
> 2½ cups regular rolled oats
> ⅓ cup coarsely chopped almonds
> ⅛ tsp kosher or sea salt
> ½ tsp ground cinnamon
> ½ cup chopped dried apricots
> 2 tbsp ground flaxseed
> ¼ cup honey
> ¼ cup extra-virgin olive oil
> 2 tsp vanilla extract

Directions:
1. Preheat the oven to 325°F. Line your large, rimmed baking sheet with parchment paper.
2. Combine the oats, almonds, salt, and cinnamon in a large skillet. Adjust to medium-high heat and cook to toast for 6 minutes, often stirring.
3. Meanwhile, in a microwave-safe bowl, combine the apricots, flaxseed, honey, and oil.
4. Microwave on high for about 1 minute or until very hot and just beginning to bubble.
5. Stir the vanilla into the honey mixture, then pour it over the oat mixture in the skillet. Stir well.
6. Spread out the granola on the prepared baking sheet. Bake for 15 minutes, until lightly browned. Remove from the oven and cool completely.
7. Break the granola into small pieces, and serve.

Nutrition: Calories: 337; Fat: 17g; Carbs: 42g; Protein: 7g

Scrambled Eggs with Goat Cheese

Ingredients:
> 1½ tsp extra-virgin olive oil
> 1 cup chopped bell peppers
> 2 garlic cloves, minced
> 6 large eggs
> ¼ tsp kosher or sea salt
> 2 tbsp water
> ½ cup crumbled goat cheese
> 2 tbsp loosely packed chopped fresh mint

Directions:
1. In your large skillet over medium-high heat, heat the oil. Add the peppers and cook for 5 minutes, stirring occasionally. Add the garlic and cook within 1 minute.
2. Meanwhile, in your medium bowl, whisk together the eggs, salt, and water.
3. Turn the heat down to medium-low. Pour the egg mixture over the peppers.
4. Let the eggs cook undisturbed for 1 to 2 minutes until they set on the bottom. Sprinkle with goat cheese.
5. Cook the eggs for about 1 to 2 more minutes, stirring slowly, until the eggs are soft-set and custardy. Top with fresh mint and serve.

4

5 minutes

3-5 minutes

Nutrition: Calories: 201; Fat: 15g; Carbs: 5g; Protein: 15g

Breakfast recipes

Almond and Maple Quick Grits

5 minutes

6-7 minutes

4

Ingredients:
- 1½ cups water
- ½ cup unsweetened almond milk
- Pinch sea salt
- ½ cup quick-cooking grits
- ½ tsp ground cinnamon
- ¼ cup pure maple syrup
- ¼ cup slivered almonds

Directions:
1. Heat the water, almond milk, and sea salt in your medium saucepan over medium-high heat until it boils.
2. Stir constantly with a wooden spoon, and slowly add the grits. Continue stirring to prevent lumps, and bring the mixture to a slow boil.
3. Adjust to medium-low heat. Simmer for 5 to 6 minutes, frequently stirring, until the water is completely absorbed.
4. Stir in the cinnamon, syrup, and almonds. Cook for 1 minute more, stirring.

Nutrition: Calories: 151; Fat: 4g; Carbs: 28g; Protein: 3g

Orange French Toast

Ingredients:
- 1½ cups unsweetened almond milk
- 2 eggs, beaten
- 2 egg whites, beaten
- 1 tsp vanilla extract
- Zest of 1 orange
- Juice of 1 orange
- 1 tsp ground nutmeg
- 6 light whole-wheat bread slices
- Nonstick cooking spray

Directions:
1. Whisk the almond milk, eggs, egg whites, vanilla, orange zest, juice, and nutmeg in your small bowl.
2. Arrange the bread in a single layer in a 9-by-13-inch baking dish. Pour the milk plus egg mixture over the top.
3. Allow the bread to soak for about 10 minutes, turning once.
4. Spray your nonstick skillet with cooking spray and heat over medium-high heat.
5. Working in batches, add the bread and cook within 5 minutes per side until the custard sets.

6

20 minutes

10 minutes

Nutrition: Calories: 223; Fat: 21g; Carbs: 15g; Protein: 8g

24 Chapter 5

CHAPTER 6
LUNCH RECIPES

Cauliflower Steaks with Olive Citrus Sauce

15 minutes

30 minutes

4

Ingredients:
> 1 or 2 large heads of cauliflower
>   cup extra-virgin olive oil
> ¼ tsp kosher salt
> ⅛ tsp ground black pepper
> Juice of 1 orange
> Zest of 1 orange
> ¼ cup black olives, pitted and chopped
> 1 tbsp Dijon or grainy mustard
> 1 tbsp red wine vinegar
> ½ tsp ground coriander

Directions:
1. Preheat the oven to 400°F. Line your baking sheet using parchment paper or foil.
2. Cut off the stem of the cauliflower so it will sit upright. Slice it vertically into four thick slabs.
3. Place the cauliflower on your baking sheet. Drizzle with olive oil, salt, and black pepper.
4. Bake for about 30 minutes, turning over once, until tender and golden brown.
5. Combine the orange juice, orange zest, olives, mustard, vinegar, and coriander in a medium bowl.
6. Serve the cauliflower warm or at room temperature with the sauce.

Nutrition: Calories: 265; Fat: 21g; Carbs: 19g; Protein: 5g

Baked Falafel Sliders

Ingredients:
> Olive oil cooking spray
> 1 (15-oz) can no-salt-added or low-sodium chickpeas, drained & rinsed
> 1 onion, roughly chopped
> 2 garlic cloves, peeled
> 2 tbsp fresh parsley, chopped
> 2 tbsp whole-wheat flour
> ½ tsp ground coriander
> ½ tsp ground cumin
> ½ tsp baking powder
> ½ tsp kosher salt
> ¼ tsp freshly ground black pepper

Directions:
1. Preheat the oven to 350°F. Line your baking sheet using parchment paper or foil and lightly spray with olive oil cooking spray.
2. Add chickpeas, onion, garlic, parsley, flour, coriander, cumin, baking powder, salt, and pepper in your food processor. Process until smooth.
3. Make 6 slider patties, each with a heaping ¼ cup of mixture, and arrange them on the prepared baking sheet.
4. Bake for 30 minutes, turning over halfway through. Serve.

6

10 minutes

30 minutes

Nutrition: Calories: 90; Fat: 1g; Carbs: 17g; Protein: 4g

26   Chapter 6

Orange-Tarragon Chicken Salad Wrap

15 minutes

0 minutes

4

Ingredients:

> ½ cup plain whole-milk Greek yogurt
> 2 tbsp Dijon mustard
> 2 tbsp extra-virgin olive oil
> 2 tbsp chopped fresh tarragon
> ½ tsp salt
> ¼ tsp freshly ground black pepper
> 2 cups cooked shredded chicken
> ½ cup slivered almonds
> 4 to 8 large Bibb lettuce leaves, tough stem removed
> 2 small ripe avocados, peeled & thinly sliced
> Zest of 1 clementine

Directions:

1. In a medium bowl, combine the yogurt, mustard, olive oil, tarragon, orange zest, salt, and pepper and whisk until creamy.
2. Add the shredded chicken and almonds and stir to coat.
3. To assemble the wraps, place about ½ cup of chicken salad mixture in the center of each lettuce leaf and top with sliced avocados.

Nutrition: Calories: 440; Fat: 32g; Carbs: 12g; Protein: 26g

Chickpeas and Kale with Spicy Pomodoro Sauce

4

10 minutes

32 minutes

Ingredients:

> 2 tbsp extra-virgin olive oil
> 4 garlic cloves, sliced
> 1 tsp red pepper flakes
> 1 (28-oz) can of no-salt-added crushed tomatoes
> 1 tsp kosher salt
> ½ tsp honey
> 1 bunch of kale, stemmed and chopped
> 2 (15-oz) cans no-salt-added or low-sodium chickpeas, drained & rinsed
> ¼ cup fresh basil, chopped
> ¼ cup grated pecorino Romano cheese

Directions:

1. Heat the olive oil in your large skillet or sauté pan over medium heat. Add the garlic and red pepper flakes, then sauté for 2 minutes until the garlic is a light golden brown.
2. Add the tomatoes, salt, and honey and mix well. Adjust to low heat and simmer for 20 minutes.
3. Add the kale and mix it well. Cook for 5 minutes. Add the chickpeas and simmer for 5 minutes.
4. Remove and stir in the basil. Serve topped with pecorino cheese.

Nutrition: Calories: 420; Fat: 13g; Carbs: 54g; Protein: 20g

Lunch recipes

Shrimp Ceviche Salad

15 minutes + marinating time

0 minutes

4

Ingredients:
> 1-pound fresh shrimp, peeled and deveined
> 1 small red or yellow bell pepper, cut into ½-inch chunks
> ½ English cucumber, peeled and cut into ½-inch chunks
> ½ small red onion, cut into thin slivers
> ¼ cup chopped fresh cilantro
>   cup freshly squeezed lime juice
> 2 tbsp freshly squeezed lemon juice
> 2 tbsp freshly squeezed clementine juice
> ½ cup extra-virgin olive oil
> 1 tsp salt
> ½ tsp freshly ground black pepper
> 2 ripe avocados, peeled, pitted, & cut into ½-inch chunks

Directions:
1. Cut the shrimp in half lengthwise. Combine the shrimp, bell pepper, cucumber, onion, and cilantro in a large glass bowl.
2. Whisk together the lime, lemon, clementine juices, olive oil, salt, and pepper in your small bowl.
3. Pour the mixture over the shrimp and veggies and toss to coat. Cover and refrigerate within 2 hours or up to 8 hours.
4. Give the mixture a toss every 30 minutes for the first 2 hours to ensure all the shrimp "cook" in the juices.
5. Add the cut avocado just before serving and toss to combine.

Nutrition: Calories: 497; Fat: 40g; Carbs: 14g; Protein: 25g

Caprese Sandwich

Ingredients:
> 2 slices Italian bread
> 1 tsp store-bought Basil Pesto
> 2 (¼-inch-thick) slices of fresh mozzarella cheese
> 1 ripe tomato, cut into ½-inch-thick slices
> ¼ cup chopped fresh basil
> ⅛ tsp salt
> ⅛ tsp freshly ground black pepper

Directions:
1. Toast the bread until lightly golden.
2. Spread ½ teaspoon of pesto on each piece of toast and place the mozzarella slices on one piece.
3. Top the cheese with the tomato and basil. Sprinkle with salt and pepper. Top with the other piece of toast and serve.

1

15 minutes

0 minutes

Nutrition: Calories: 345; Fat: 18g; Carbs: 27g; Protein: 19g

Crispy Mediterranean Chicken Thighs

Ingredients:
> 2 tbsp extra-virgin olive oil
> 2 tsp dried rosemary
> 1½ tsp ground cumin
> 1½ tsp ground coriander
> ¾ tsp dried oregano
> ⅛ tsp salt
> 6 bone-in, skin-on chicken thighs

Directions:
1. Preheat the oven to 450°F. Line a baking sheet with parchment paper.
2. Place the olive oil and spices into a large bowl and mix, making a paste.
3. Add the chicken and mix until evenly coated. Place on the prepared baking sheet.
4. Bake within 30 to 35 minutes until golden brown and the chicken registers an internal temperature of 165°F.

5 minutes

30-35 minutes

6

Nutrition: Calories: 440; Fat: 34g; Carbs: 1g; Protein: 30g

Swiss Chard and Black-Eyed Pea Pilaf

Ingredients:
> 10 cups water, divided
> 1-pound Swiss chard, or kale, chopped
> ¼ cup olive oil
> 1 onion, chopped
> 1 cup canned black-eyed peas, drained and rinsed (see tip)
> 1 garlic clove, mashed
> ½ teaspoon ground coriander
> 1 cup coarse bulgur #3

Directions:
1. In your large soup pot over medium heat, boil 8 cups of water. Add the Swiss chard and return it to a boil.
2. Cook for 5 minutes. Remove from the heat, drain, and set aside to cool. Return the soup pot to medium heat and add the olive oil to warm.
3. Add the onion and cook within 5 minutes. Add the black-eyed peas and cook for 10 minutes more.
4. Stir in the garlic, coriander, and Swiss chard. Cook for 1 minute.
5. Pour the remaining 2 cups of water over the vegetables, increase the heat, and bring the mixture to a boil.
6. Add the bulgur and return everything to a boil. Adjust to medium-low heat, cover, and cook for 10 minutes.
7. Turn off the heat and let the pilaf rest for 10 minutes before serving.

4

20 minutes

35-40 minutes

Nutrition: Calories: 307; Fat: 14g; Carbs: 42g; Protein: 10g

Lunch recipes   29

Pistachio Mint Pesto Pasta

10 minutes

10 minutes

4

Ingredients:
- 8 oz whole-wheat pasta
- 1 cup fresh mint
- ½ cup fresh basil
- cup unsalted pistachios shelled
- 1 garlic clove, peeled
- ½ tsp kosher salt
- Juice of ½ lime
- cup extra-virgin olive oil

Directions:
1. Cook the pasta as stated in the package directions. Drain, reserving ½ cup of the pasta water, and set aside.
2. Add the mint, basil, pistachios, garlic, salt, and lime juice to a food processor.
3. Process until the pistachios are coarsely ground. Add the olive oil in your slow, steady stream and process until incorporated.
4. In your large bowl, mix the pasta with the pistachio pesto; toss well to incorporate.
5. If a thinner, more saucy consistency is desired, add some of the reserved pasta water and toss well.

Nutrition: Calories: 420; Fat: 3g; Carbs: 48g; Protein: 11g

Crab Cake Lettuce Cups

Ingredients:
- 1-pound jumbo lump crab
- 1 large egg
- 6 tbsp avocado oil mayonnaise, divided
- 2 tbsp Dijon mustard
- ½ cup almond flour
- ¼ cup minced red onion
- 2 tsp smoked paprika
- 1 tsp celery salt
- 1 tsp garlic powder
- 1 tsp dried dill (optional)
- ½ tsp freshly ground black pepper
- ¼ cup extra-virgin olive oil
- 4 large Bibb lettuce leaves, thick spine removed

Directions:
1. Place the crabmeat in your large bowl, pick out any visible shells, then break apart the meat with a fork.
2. Whisk together the egg, 2 tbsp avocado oil mayonnaise, and Dijon mustard in your small bowl. Add to the crabmeat and blend with a fork.
3. Add the almond flour, red onion, paprika, celery salt, garlic powder, dill (if using), and pepper and combine well. Let it sit at room temperature for 10 to 15 minutes.
4. Form into 8 small cakes, about 2 inches in diameter.
5. In your large skillet, heat the olive oil over medium-high heat. Fry the cakes for 2 to 3 minutes per side until browned.
6. Cover the skillet, adjust to low heat, and cook for another 6 to 8 minutes or until set in the center. Remove from the skillet.
7. To serve, wrap 2 small crab cakes in each lettuce leaf and top with 1 tablespoon of avocado oil mayonnaise.

4

20 min + marinating time

10-14 minutes

Nutrition: Calories: 344; Fat: 24g; Carbs: 8g; Protein: 24g

Chapter 6

Harissa Yogurt Chicken Thighs

5 minutes + marinating time

22-23 minutes

4

Ingredients:
> ½ cup plain Greek yogurt
> 2 tbsp harissa
> 1 tbsp lemon juice
> ½ tsp kosher salt
> ¼ tsp freshly ground black pepper
> 1½ pounds boneless, skinless chicken thighs

Directions:
1. Combine the yogurt, harissa, lemon juice, salt, and black pepper in a bowl. Add the chicken and mix again.
2. Marinate in your refrigerator for at least 15 minutes and up to 4 hours.
3. Preheat the oven to 425°F. Line your baking sheet using parchment paper or foil. Arrange the marinated chicken thighs in one layer on the baking sheet. Roast for 20 minutes, turning the chicken over halfway.
4. Change the oven temperature to broil. Broil the chicken for 2 to 3 minutes until golden brown in spots.

Nutrition: Calories: 190; Fat: 10g; Carbs: 1g; Protein: 24g

Herbed Ricotta-Stuffed Mushrooms

4

10 minutes

30-35 minutes

Ingredients:
> 6 tbsp extra-virgin olive oil, divided
> 4 portobello mushroom caps were cleaned & gills removed
> 1 cup whole-milk ricotta cheese
> ⅓ cup chopped fresh herbs
> 2 garlic cloves, finely minced
> ½ tsp salt
> ¼ tsp freshly ground black pepper

Directions:
1. Preheat the oven to 400°F.
2. Line your baking sheet with parchment or foil and drizzle with 2 tablespoons olive oil, spreading evenly.
3. Place the mushroom caps on the baking sheet, gill-side up.
4. Mix the ricotta, herbs, 2 tablespoons olive oil, garlic, salt, and pepper in your medium bowl.
5. Stuff each mushroom cap with one-quarter of the cheese mixture, pressing down if needed.
6. Drizzle with remaining olive oil, then bake for 30 to 35 minutes until golden brown and the mushrooms are soft.

Nutrition: Calories: 285; Fat: 25g; Carbs: 8g; Protein: 7g

Lunch recipes

Citrus-Glazed Salmon with Zucchini Noodles

Ingredients:
- 4 (5- to 6-oz) pieces of salmon
- ½ tsp kosher salt
- ¼ tsp freshly ground black pepper
- 1 tbsp extra-virgin olive oil
- 1 cup freshly squeezed orange juice
- 1 tsp low-sodium soy sauce
- 2 zucchini (about 16 ounces), spiralized
- 1 tbsp fresh chives, chopped
- 1 tbsp fresh parsley, chopped

Directions:
1. Preheat the oven to 350°F. Season the salmon with salt and black pepper.
2. Heat the olive oil in your large oven-safe skillet or sauté pan over medium-high heat.
3. Add the salmon, skin-side down, and sear within 5 minutes until crispy.
4. Turn the salmon over and transfer to the oven for 7 minutes until your desired doneness is reached. Place the salmon on a cutting board to rest.
5. Place the same pan on the stove over medium-high heat. Add the orange juice and soy sauce to deglaze the pan.
6. Let it simmer, scraping up any brown bits, and continue to simmer for 5 to 7 minutes until the liquid is reduced by half to a syrup-like consistency.
7. Divide the zucchini noodles among 4 plates and place 1 piece of salmon on each.
8. Pour the orange glaze over the salmon and zucchini noodles. Garnish with chives and parsley.

10 minutes
17-19 minutes
4

Nutrition: Calories: 280; Fat: 13g; Carbs: 11g; Protein: 30g

Cauliflower Tabbouleh Salad

Ingredients:
- ¼ cup extra-virgin olive oil
- ¼ cup lemon juice
- Zest of 1 lemon
- ¾ tsp kosher salt
- ½ tsp ground turmeric
- ¼ tsp ground coriander
- ¼ tsp ground cumin
- ¼ tsp black pepper
- ⅛ tsp ground cinnamon
- 1-pound riced cauliflower
- 1 English cucumber, diced
- 12 cherry tomatoes, halved
- 1 cup fresh parsley, chopped
- ½ cup fresh mint, chopped

Directions:
1. Whisk the olive oil, lemon juice, zest, salt, turmeric, coriander, cumin, black pepper, and cinnamon in your large bowl.
2. Add the riced cauliflower to the bowl and mix well. Add the cucumber, tomatoes, parsley, and mint, and gently mix again.

4
15 minutes
0 minutes

Nutrition: Calories: 180; Fat: 15g; Carbs: 12g; Protein: 4g

32 Chapter 6

Yogurt-Marinated Chicken Kebabs

Ingredients:

- ½ cup plain Greek yogurt
- 1 tbsp lemon juice
- ½ tsp ground cumin
- ½ tsp ground coriander
- ½ tsp kosher salt
- ¼ tsp cayenne pepper
- 1½ pound chicken breast, skinless & boneless, cut into 1-inch cubes

Directions:

1. Combine the yogurt, lemon juice, cumin, coriander, salt, and cayenne pepper in a large bowl or zip-top bag.
2. Mix thoroughly and then add the chicken—Marinate within 30 minutes and up to overnight in the refrigerator.
3. Preheat the oven to 425°F. Line your baking sheet using parchment paper or foil.
4. Thread the marinated chicken on 4 bamboo or metal skewers.
5. Bake for 20 minutes, turning the chicken over once halfway through the cooking time.

10 minutes + marinating time

20 minutes

4

Nutrition: Calories: 170; Fat: 4g; Carbs: 1g; Protein: 31g

Lunch recipes   33

CHAPTER 7
DINNER RECIPES

Tuscan Bean Soup with Kale

10 minutes

20-21 minutes

4

Ingredients:
> 2 tbsp extra-virgin olive oil
> 1 onion, diced
> 1 carrot, diced
> 1 celery stalk, diced
> 1 tsp kosher salt
> 4 cups no-salt-added vegetable stock
> 1 (15-oz) can of no-salt-added or low-sodium cannellini beans, drained & rinsed
> 1 tbsp fresh thyme, chopped
> 1 tbsp fresh sage, chopped
> 1 tbsp fresh oregano, chopped
> ¼ tsp freshly ground black pepper
> 1 bunch of kale, stemmed and chopped
> ¼ cup grated Parmesan cheese (optional)

Directions:
1. Heat the olive oil in your large pot over medium-high heat. Add the onion, carrot, celery, and salt and sauté for 5 to 6 minutes until translucent and slightly golden.
2. Add the vegetable stock, beans, thyme, sage, oregano, and black pepper. Let it boil.
3. Adjust to low heat, and simmer for 10 minutes. Mix in the kale and wilt for 5 minutes.
4. Sprinkle 1 tablespoon Parmesan cheese over each bowl before serving, if desired.

Nutrition: Calories: 235; Fat: 8g; Carbs: 35g; Protein: 9g

Garlicky Shrimp with Mushrooms

4

10 minutes

11-13 minutes

Ingredients:
> 1 pound peeled & deveined fresh shrimp
> 1 tsp salt
> 1 cup extra-virgin olive oil
> 8 large garlic cloves, thinly sliced
> 4 oz sliced mushrooms of your choice
> ½ tsp red pepper flakes
> ¼ cup chopped fresh flat-leaf Italian parsley

Directions:
1. Rinse the shrimp and pat dry. Place in a small bowl and sprinkle with salt.
2. In a large rimmed, thick skillet, heat the olive oil over medium-low heat.
3. Add the garlic and heat for 3 to 4 minutes until very fragrant, reducing the heat if the garlic starts to burn.
4. Add the mushrooms and sauté for 5 minutes, until softened.
5. Add the shrimp and red pepper flakes and sauté for another 3 to 4 minutes until the shrimp turns pink. Remove and stir in the parsley. Serve.

Nutrition: Calories: 620; Fat: 56g; Carbs: 4g; Protein: 24g

Dinner recipes

Braised Short Ribs with Red Wine

10 minutes

1½ to 2 hours

4

Ingredients:
> 1½ pounds boneless beef short ribs
> 1 tsp salt
> ½ tsp freshly ground black pepper
> ½ tsp garlic powder
> ¼ cup extra-virgin olive oil
> 1 cup dry red wine
> 2 to 3 cups of beef broth divided
> 4 sprigs rosemary

Directions:
1. Preheat the oven to 350°F.
2. Flavor the short ribs with salt, pepper, and garlic powder. Let it sit for 10 minutes.
3. Heat the oil over medium-high heat in a Dutch oven or oven-safe deep skillet.
4. Add the short ribs and brown until dark in color, 2 to 3 minutes per side. Remove the meat from the oil and keep it warm.
5. Add the red wine and 2 cups of beef broth to the Dutch oven, whisk together, and let it boil.
6. Adjust to low heat and simmer for 10 minutes until the liquid is lessened to about 2 cups.
7. Return the short ribs to the liquid, which should come halfway up the meat, adding up to 1 cup of remaining broth if needed.
8. Cover and braise for 1½ to 2 hours until the meat is tender.
9. Remove and let it sit for 10 minutes, covered, before serving. Serve warm, drizzled with cooking liquid.

Nutrition: Calories: 792; Fat: 76g; Carbs: 2g; Protein: 25g

Ratatouille

Ingredients:
> ¼ cup olive oil
> 1 onion, chopped
> 4 garlic cloves, crushed
> 1 large eggplant, cut into 1-inch cubes
> 1 zucchini, cut into 1-inch cubes
> 1 red bell pepper, seeded & chopped
> ⅛ tsp salt, + more as needed
> 3 tomatoes, chopped
> 1 tbsp dried oregano
> 1 tsp dried thyme
> ¼ cup chopped fresh basil

Directions:
1. In a heavy-bottomed skillet over medium heat, heat the olive oil.
2. Add the onion and cook within 5 minutes or until soft. Add the garlic and cook within 2 minutes.
3. Add the eggplant and cook for 10 minutes, stirring often. Stir in the zucchini, red bell pepper, and salt. Cook for 5 minutes.
4. Stir in the tomatoes, oregano, thyme, and basil. Cook for 10 minutes. Taste and season with more salt as needed.

4

20 minutes

32 minutes

Nutrition: Calories: 191; Fat: 13g; Carbs: 19g; Protein: 4g

36 Chapter 7

Burst Cherry Tomato Sauce with Angel Hair

Ingredients:
- 8 oz angel hair pasta
- 2 tbsp extra-virgin olive oil
- 3 garlic cloves, minced
- 3 pints cherry tomatoes
- ½ tsp kosher salt
- ¼ tsp red pepper flakes
- ¾ cup fresh basil, chopped
- 1 tbsp white balsamic vinegar (optional)
- ¼ cup grated Parmesan cheese (optional)

Directions:
1. Cook the pasta as stated in the package directions. Drain and set aside.
2. Heat the olive oil in your skillet or large sauté pan over medium-high heat. Add the garlic and sauté within 30 seconds.
3. Add the tomatoes, salt, and red pepper flakes and cook within 15 minutes, often stirring, until the tomatoes burst.
4. Remove from the heat and add the pasta and basil. Toss together well. Serve with the grated Parmesan cheese, if desired.

10 minutes
20 minutes
4

Nutrition: Calories: 305; Fat: 8g; Carbs: 53g; Protein: 11g

Moroccan Stuffed Peppers

Ingredients:
- ¼ cup + 2 tbsp extra-virgin olive oil, divided
- 2 large red bell peppers
- 1 pound ground beef
- 1 small onion, finely chopped
- 2 garlic cloves, minced
- 2 tbsp chopped fresh sage o
- 1 tsp salt
- 1 tsp ground allspice
- ½ tsp freshly ground black pepper
- ½ cup chopped fresh flat-leaf Italian parsley
- ½ cup chopped baby arugula leaves
- ½ cup chopped walnuts
- 1 tbsp freshly squeezed orange juice

Directions:
1. Preheat the oven to 425°F.
2. Drizzle 1 tablespoon olive oil on a rimmed baking sheet and swirl to coat the bottom.
3. Remove the stems from the peppers and cut them in half, then remove the seeds and membranes.
4. Place cut-side down on the prepared baking sheet and roast for 5 to 8 minutes until just softened. Remove and allow to cool.
5. Meanwhile, in your large skillet, heat 1 tbsp olive oil over medium-high heat.
6. Add the beef and onions and sauté within 8 to 10 minutes until the beef is browned and cooked through.
7. Add the garlic, sage, salt, allspice, and pepper and sauté for 2 more minutes.
8. Remove from the heat and cool slightly. Stir in the parsley, arugula, walnuts, orange juice, and remaining olive oil.
9. Stuff the filling into each pepper half. Return to the oven and cook for 5 minutes. Serve warm.

4
15 minutes
20-25 minutes

Nutrition: Calories: 521; Fat: 44g; Carbs: 9g; Protein: 25g

Dinner recipes

Salmon with Tarragon-Dijon Sauce

15 minutes
10-12 minutes
4

Ingredients:

> 1¼ pounds salmon fillet (skin on or removed), cut into 4 equal pieces
> ¼ cup avocado oil mayonnaise
> ¼ cup Dijon or stone-ground mustard
> Zest & juice of ½ lemon
> 2 tbsp chopped fresh tarragon
> ½ tsp salt
> ¼ tsp freshly ground black pepper
> 4 tbsp extra-virgin olive oil for serving

Directions:

1. Preheat the oven to 425°F. Line a baking sheet with parchment paper.
2. Place the salmon pieces, skin-side down, on a baking sheet.
3. Whisk the mayonnaise, mustard, lemon zest, juice, tarragon, salt, and pepper in your small bowl. Top the salmon evenly with the sauce mixture.
4. Bake for 10 to 12 minutes until slightly browned on top and slightly translucent in the center.
5. Remove and leave on your baking sheet for 10 minutes. Drizzle each fillet with 1 tablespoon of olive oil before serving.

Nutrition: Calories: 387; Fat: 28g; Carbs: 4g; Protein: 29g

Vegetable Paella

6
20 minutes
45 minutes

Ingredients:

> ¼ cup olive oil
> 1 large sweet onion, chopped
> 1 large red bell pepper, seeded & chopped
> 1 large green bell pepper, seeded & chopped
> 3 garlic cloves, finely minced
> 1 tsp smoked paprika
> 5 saffron threads
> 1 zucchini, cut into ½-inch cubes
> 4 large ripe tomatoes, peeled, seeded, & chopped
> 1½ cups short-grain Spanish rice
> 3 cups vegetable broth, warmed

Directions:

1. Preheat the oven to 350°F.
2. Heat the olive oil in your paella pan or large oven-safe skillet over medium heat. Add the onion and red and green bell peppers and cook for 10 minutes.
3. Stir in the garlic, paprika, saffron threads, zucchini, and tomatoes. Adjust to medium-low heat and cook for 10 minutes.
4. Stir in the rice and vegetable broth. Increase the heat to bring the paella to a boil.
5. Adjust to medium-low heat and cook for 15 minutes. Cover the pan with aluminum foil and put it in the oven.
6. Bake for 10 minutes or until the broth is absorbed. Serve.

Nutrition: Calories: 288; Fat: 10g; Carbs: 46g; Protein: 5g

Chapter 7

Lentil And Mushroom Lasagna

20 minutes

35 minutes

4

Ingredients:

- 2 cups dried brown lentils, rinsed and picked over for debris
- 6 cups water
- ¼ cup olive oil
- 1 onion, finely chopped
- 4 garlic cloves, minced
- 1-pound white mushrooms, cut into slices
- ½ cup chopped fresh cilantro
- 4 cups store-bought Tomato Basil Sauce, divided
- ⅛ tsp salt, + more as needed
- ⅛ tsp freshly ground black pepper, + more as needed
- 1 (9-oz) package of no-boil lasagna sheets
- 1 cup shredded fresh mozzarella cheese

Directions:

1. Preheat the oven to 400°F.
2. In your large saucepan over high heat, combine the lentils and water. Let it boil.
3. Adjust to medium-low heat and cook for 10 minutes until the lentils are tender. Drain and set aside.
4. Heat the olive oil in your sauté pan or skillet over medium heat.
5. Add the onion and cook within 5 minutes. Stir in the garlic, mushrooms, and cilantro. Cook for 5 minutes.
6. Stir in the lentils, 2 cups of tomato sauce, salt, and pepper—season with salt and pepper. Remove from the heat.
7. Spoon and spread 1 cup of tomato sauce over the bottom of your 9-by-13-inch baking dish. Cover the sauce using a layer of lasagna sheets.
8. Spoon and spread the lentil mixture evenly over the lasagna. Cover the lentils with a layer of lasagna sheets.
9. Pour the remaining tomato sauce over the lasagna sheets. Bake for 15 minutes.
10. Sprinkle with the mozzarella cheese and bake for 5 minutes more or until the cheese is browned and bubbling.

Nutrition: Calories: 410; Fat: 12g; Carbs: 53g; Protein: 25g

Dinner recipes

Greek Stuffed Squid

Ingredients:
- 8 oz frozen spinach, thawed & drained
- 4 oz crumbled goat cheese
- ½ cup chopped pitted olives
- ½ cup extra-virgin olive oil, divided
- ¼ cup chopped sun-dried tomatoes
- ¼ cup chopped fresh flat-leaf Italian parsley
- 2 garlic cloves, finely minced
- ¼ tsp freshly ground black pepper
- 2 pounds baby squid, cleaned & tentacles removed

Directions:
1. Preheat the oven to 350°F.
2. Combine the spinach, goat cheese, olives, ¼ cup olive oil, sun-dried tomatoes, parsley, garlic, and pepper in a medium bowl.
3. Pour 2 tablespoons olive oil into the bottom of an 8-inch square baking dish and spread to coat the bottom.
4. Stuff each cleaned squid with 2 to 3 tablespoons of cheese mixture and place in the prepared baking dish.
5. Drizzle the tops with the remaining olive oil and bake within 25 to 30 minutes until the squid is cooked through.
6. Remove and allow to cool for 5 to 10 minutes before serving.

15 minutes

25-30 minutes

4

Nutrition: Calories: 469; Fat: 37g; Carbs: 10g; Protein: 24g

French Bean Stew

Ingredients:
- ¼ cup olive oil
- 1 onion, chopped
- 1-pound French green beans, trimmed & cut into 2-inch pieces
- 4 ripe tomatoes, seeded and diced
- 4 garlic cloves, minced
- ⅛ tsp salt
- ⅛ tsp freshly ground black pepper
- 2 tbsp tomato paste
- 2 cups vegetable broth

Directions:
1. In your soup pot over medium heat, heat the olive oil. Add the onion and cook within 5 minutes, often stirring, until softened.
2. Add the green beans, cover the pot, and cook for 10 minutes, stirring often.
3. Stir in the tomatoes and their juices, garlic, salt, and pepper. Cook for 10 minutes.
4. Whisk the tomato paste and vegetable broth in a medium bowl until completely combined. Pour the broth into the pot.
5. Let the stew boil. Cover and simmer for 15 minutes—season with more salt and pepper, as needed, before serving.

4

10 minutes

30 minutes

Nutrition: Calories: 207; Fat: 14g; Carbs: 18g; Protein: 6g

Pan-Fried Pork Chops with Onions

10 minutes
16-21 minutes
4

Ingredients:
> 4 (4-oz) pork chops, untrimmed
> 1½ tsp salt, divided
> 1 tsp freshly ground black pepper, divided
> ½ cup extra-virgin olive oil, divided
> 1 red or orange bell pepper, thinly sliced
> 1 green bell pepper, thinly sliced
> 1 small yellow onion, thinly sliced
> 2 tsp dried Italian herbs
> 2 garlic cloves, minced
> 1 tbsp balsamic vinegar

Directions:
1. Flavor the pork chops with 1 tsp salt and ½ tsp pepper.
2. In a large skillet, heat ¼ cup olive oil over medium-high heat. Fry the pork chops for 4 to 5 minutes per side until browned. Remove and cover to keep warm.
3. Pour the remaining olive oil into the skillet and sauté the sliced peppers, onions, and herbs for 6 to 8 minutes over medium-high heat until tender.
4. Add the garlic, stirring to combine, and return the pork to the skillet. Cover, adjust to low heat, and cook for another 2 to 3 minutes or until the pork is cooked through.
5. Turn off the heat. Transfer the pork, peppers, and onions to a serving platter using a slotted spoon.
6. Add the vinegar to the oil in the skillet and whisk to combine well. Drizzle the vinaigrette over the pork and serve warm.

Nutrition: Calories: 508; Fat: 40g; Carbs: 8g; Protein: 31g

Roasted Eggplant Soup

6
15 minutes
40 minutes

Ingredients:
> Olive oil cooking spray
> 2 pounds (1 to 2 medium to large) eggplant, halved lengthwise
> 2 beefsteak tomatoes, halved
> 2 onions, halved
> 4 garlic cloves smashed
> 4 rosemary sprigs
> 2 tbsp extra-virgin olive oil
> 1 to 2 cups of no-salt-added vegetable stock
> 1 tsp pure maple syrup
> 1 tsp ground cumin
> 1 tsp ground coriander
> 1 tsp kosher salt
> ¼ tsp freshly ground black pepper

Directions:
1. Preheat the oven to 400°F—line two baking sheets using parchment paper or foil. Lightly spray with olive oil cooking spray.
2. Spread the eggplant, tomatoes, onions, and garlic on the prepared baking sheets, cut-side down. Nestle the rosemary sprigs among the vegetables.
3. Drizzle with the olive oil and roast for 40 minutes, checking halfway through and removing the garlic before it gets brown.
4. When cool enough to touch, remove the eggplant flesh and tomato flesh from the skin and add to a high-powered blender.
5. Add the rosemary leaves, onions, garlic, 1 cup of vegetable stock, maple syrup, cumin, coriander, salt, and black pepper. Purée until smooth. Serve.

Nutrition: Calories: 185; Fat: 8g; Carbs: 29g; Protein: 4g

Dinner recipes

Flounder with Tomatoes and Basil

Ingredients:
- 1 pound cherry tomatoes
- 4 garlic cloves, sliced
- 2 tbsp extra-virgin olive oil
- 2 tbsp lemon juice
- 2 tbsp basil, cut into ribbons
- ½ tsp kosher salt
- ¼ tsp freshly ground black pepper
- 4 (5- to 6-oz) flounder fillets

Directions:
1. Preheat the oven to 425°F.
2. Combine the tomatoes, garlic, olive oil, lemon juice, basil, salt, and black pepper in a baking dish. Bake for 5 minutes.
3. Remove the baking dish and arrange the flounder on the tomato mixture.
4. Bake for 10 to 15 minutes until the fish is opaque and flakes.

10 minutes

15-20 minutes

4

Nutrition: Calories: 215; Fat: 9g; Carbs: 6g; Protein: 28g

Greek Turkey Burger

Ingredients:
- 1 pound ground turkey
- 1 medium zucchini, grated
- ¼ cup whole-wheat bread crumbs
- ¼ cup red onion, minced
- ¼ cup crumbled feta cheese
- 1 large egg, beaten
- 1 garlic clove, minced
- 1 tbsp fresh oregano, chopped
- 1 tsp kosher salt
- ¼ tsp freshly ground black pepper
- 1 tbsp extra-virgin olive oil

Directions:
1. Combine the turkey, zucchini, bread crumbs, onion, feta cheese, egg, garlic, oregano, salt, and black pepper in a large bowl. Shape into 4 equal patties.
2. Heat the olive oil in your large nonstick grill pan or skillet over medium-high heat.
3. Add the burgers to the pan and adjust to medium heat. Cook on one side for 5 minutes, then flip and cook the other side for 5 minutes more.

4

10 minutes

10 minutes

Nutrition: Calories: 285; Fat: 16g; Carbs: 9g; Protein: 26g

Chapter 7

CHAPTER 8
SNACK IDEAS

Citrus-Marinated Olives

Ingredients:
- 2 cups mixed green olives with pits
- ¼ cup red wine vinegar
- ¼ cup extra-virgin olive oil
- 4 garlic cloves, finely minced
- Zest and juice of 2 clementines
- 1 tsp red pepper flakes
- 2 bay leaves
- ½ tsp ground cumin
- ½ tsp ground allspice

Directions:
1. Combine the olives, vinegar, oil, garlic, orange zest and juice, red pepper flakes, bay leaves, cumin, and allspice in a large glass bowl or jar.
2. Cover and refrigerate within 4 hours or up to a week to allow the olives to marinate, tossing again before serving.

5 minutes + marinating time

0 minutes

2

Nutrition: Calories: 133; Fat: 14g; Carbs: 3g; Protein: 1g

Manchego Crackers

Ingredients:
- 4 tbsp butter at room temperature
- 1 cup finely shredded Manchego cheese
- 1 cup almond flour
- 1 tsp salt, divided
- ¼ tsp freshly ground black pepper
- 1 large egg

Directions:
1. Cream the butter and shredded cheese using your electric mixer until well combined and smooth.
2. Combine the almond flour with ½ teaspoon salt and pepper in your small bowl.
3. Slowly add the almond flour mixture to the cheese, constantly mixing until the dough comes together to form a ball.
4. Transfer to a piece of parchment or plastic wrap and roll into a cylinder log about 1½ inches thick. Wrap tightly and refrigerate for at least 1 hour.
5. Preheat the oven to 350°F—line two baking sheets using parchment paper or silicone baking mats.
6. To make the egg wash, whisk together the egg and the remaining salt in a small bowl.
7. Slice the refrigerated dough into small rounds, about ¼ inch thick, and place on the lined baking sheets.
8. Brush the tops of the crackers with egg wash and bake for 12 to 15 minutes until the crackers are golden and crispy.
9. Remove and allow to cool on a wire rack. Serve warm.

40

15 min + chilling time

12-15 minutes

Nutrition: Calories: 243; Fat: 23g; Carbs: 1g; Protein: 8g

Cherry Tomato Bruschetta

Ingredients:

> 8 ounces assorted cherry tomatoes, halved
>   cup fresh herbs, chopped (such as basil, parsley, tarragon, dill)
> 1 tbsp extra-virgin olive oil
> ¼ tsp kosher salt
> ⅛ tsp freshly ground black pepper
> ¼ cup ricotta cheese
> 4 slices whole-wheat bread, toasted

Directions:

1. Combi ne the tomatoes, herbs, olive oil, salt, and black pepper in a medium bowl.
2. Spread 1 tablespoon of ricotta cheese onto each slice of toast. Spoon one-quarter of the tomato mixture onto each bruschetta. If desired, garnish with more herbs.

15 minutes
0 minutes
4

Nutrition: Calories: 100; Fat: 6g; Carbs: 10g; Protein: 4g

Smoked Salmon Crudités

Ingredients:

> 6 oz smoked wild salmon
> 2 tbsp avocado mayonnaise
> 1 tbsp Dijon mustard
> 1 tbsp chopped scallions, green parts only
> 2 tsp chopped capers
> ½ tsp dried dill
> 4 endive spears or hearts of romaine
> ½ English cucumber, cut into ¼-inch-thick rounds

Directions:

1. Roughly chop the smoked salmon and place it in a small bowl. Add the avocado mayonnaise, Dijon, scallions, capers, and dill, and mix well.
2. Top endive spears and cucumber rounds with a spoonful of the smoked salmon mixture, and enjoy chilled.

4
10 minutes
0 minutes

Nutrition: Calories: 92; Fat: 5g; Carbs: 5g; Protein: 9g

Snack ideas   45

Greek Deviled Eggs

Ingredients:
> 4 large hardboiled eggs, peeled
> 2 tbsp whole-milk Greek yogurt
> ½ cup finely crumbled feta cheese
> 8 pitted Kalamata olives, finely chopped
> 2 tbsp chopped sun-dried tomatoes
> 1 tbsp minced red onion
> ½ tsp dried dill
> ¼ tsp freshly ground black pepper

Directions:
1. Slice the hardboiled eggs in half lengthwise, remove the yolks, and place it in your medium bowl. Reserve the egg white halves and set them aside.
2. Smash the yolks well with a fork. Add the yogurt, feta, olives, sun-dried tomatoes, onion, dill, and pepper, and stir until smooth and creamy.
3. Spoon the filling into each egg white half and chill for 30 minutes, or up to 24 hours, covered.

15 minutes + chilling time
15 minutes
4

Nutrition: Calories: 147; Fat: 11g; Carbs: 3g; Protein: 9g

Spiced Maple Nuts

Ingredients:
> 2 cups raw walnuts or pecans (or a mix of nuts)
> 1 tsp extra-virgin olive oil
> 1 tsp ground sumac
> ½ tsp pure maple syrup
> ¼ tsp kosher salt
> ¼ tsp ground ginger
> 2 to 4 rosemary sprigs

Directions:
1. Preheat the oven to 350°F. Line your baking sheet using parchment paper or foil.
2. Combine the nuts, olive oil, sumac, maple syrup, salt, and ginger in a large bowl.
3. Spread in one layer on the prepared baking sheet. Add the rosemary—Roast for 8 to 10 minutes or until golden and fragrant.
4. Remove the rosemary leaves from the stems and place them in a serving bowl. Add the nuts and toss to combine before serving.

2
5 minutes
8-10 minutes

Nutrition: Calories: 175; Fat: 18g; Carbs: 4g; Protein: 3g

46 Chapter 8

Marinated Feta and Artichokes

Ingredients:
- 4 oz traditional Greek feta, cut into ½-inch cubes
- 4 oz drained artichoke hearts, quartered lengthwise
- ⅓ cup extra-virgin olive oil
- Zest and juice of 1 lemon
- 2 tbsp roughly chopped fresh rosemary
- 2 tbsp roughly chopped fresh parsley
- ½ tsp black peppercorns

Directions:
1. Combine the feta and artichoke hearts in a glass bowl or large glass jar.
2. Add the olive oil, lemon zest, juice, rosemary, parsley, and peppercorns, and toss gently to coat, ensuring not to crumble the feta.
3. Cover and refrigerate within 4 hours or up to 4 days. Pull out of the refrigerator 30 minutes before serving.

5 minutes + chilling time

0 minutes

1½

Nutrition: Calories: 235; Fat: 23g; Carbs: 3g; Protein: 4g

Burrata Caprese Stack

Ingredients:
- 1 large organic tomato, preferably an heirloom
- ½ tsp salt
- ¼ tsp freshly ground black pepper
- 1 (4-oz) ball of burrata cheese
- 8 fresh basil leaves, thinly sliced
- 2 tbsp extra-virgin olive oil
- 1 tbsp red wine or balsamic vinegar

Directions:
1. Slice the tomato into 4 thick slices, remove any tough center core, and sprinkle with salt and pepper. Place the tomatoes, seasoned-side up, on a plate.
2. On a separate rimmed plate, slice the burrata into 4 thick slices and place one slice on top of each tomato slice.
3. Top each with one-quarter of the basil, and pour any reserved burrata cream from the rimmed plate over the top.
4. Drizzle with olive oil and vinegar and serve with a fork and knife.

4

5 minutes

0 minutes

Nutrition: Calories: 153; Fat: 13g; Carbs: 2g; Protein: 7g

Snack ideas

Pistachio-Stuffed Dates

Ingredients:
- ½ cup unsalted pistachios shelled
- ¼ tsp kosher salt
- 8 Medjool dates, pitted

Directions:
1. In your food processor, add the pistachios and salt. Process until combined with chunky nut butter, 3 to 5 minutes.
2. Split open the dates and spoon the pistachio nut butter into each half.

10 minutes

0 minutes

4

Nutrition: Calories: 220; Fat: 7g; Carbs: 41g; Protein: 4g

Roasted Za'atar Chickpeas

Ingredients:
- 3 tbsp za'atar
- 2 tbsp unrefined olive oil
- ½ tsp kosher salt
- ¼ tsp freshly ground black pepper
- 4 cups rinsed and drained cooked beans

Directions:
1. Set the oven to 400°F. Use foil or parchment paper to line your baking tray.
2. In a sizable dish, mix the za'atar, olive oil, salt, and black pepper. After fully combining, add the chickpeas.
3. On the prepared baking tray, distribute the chickpeas in a single layer. Bake for 45 to 60 minutes or until crisp and browned. Chill, then dish.

8

5 minutes

60 minutes

Nutrition: Calories: 150; Fat: 6g; Carbs: 17g; Protein: 6g

CHAPTER 9
SWEET DESSERTS

Strawberry Panna Cotta

Ingredients:
> 2 tbsp warm water
> 2 tsp gelatin powder
> 2 cups heavy cream
> 1 cup sliced strawberries, plus more for garnish
> 1 to 2 tbsp sugar-free sweetener of choice (optional)
> 1½ tsp pure vanilla extract
> 4 to 6 fresh mint leaves for garnish (optional)

Directions:
1. Pour the warm water into a small bowl. Sprinkle the gelatin over the water and stir well to dissolve. Allow the mixture to sit for 10 minutes.
2. In a blender or a large bowl, if using an immersion blender, combine the cream, strawberries, sweetener (if using), and vanilla.
3. Blend until smooth and the strawberries are well puréed.
4. Transfer the mixture to a saucepan and heat over medium-low heat until just below a simmer. Remove from the heat and cool for 5 minutes.
5. Whisking constantly, add in the gelatin mixture until smooth. Divide the custard between ramekins or small glass bowls, cover, and refrigerate until set, 4 to 6 hours.
6. Serve chilled, garnishing with additional sliced strawberries or mint leaves (if using).

10 minutes + chilling time
10 minutes
4

Nutrition: Calories: 431; Fat: 44g; Carbs: 7g; Protein: 4g

Clafoutis

Ingredients:
> 3 tbsp melted butter at room temperature, + more for greasing
> ½ cup all-purpose flour
> ½ cup sugar
> ¼ tsp salt
> 3 large eggs
> Grated zest of 2 lemons
> ⅓ cup whole milk
> 3 cups cherries, pitted
> 1 tbsp powdered sugar for serving

Directions:
1. Preheat the oven to 350°F. Coat a 9-inch round baking pan with butter. Set aside.
2. In a medium bowl, whisk the flour, sugar, and salt. Set aside.
3. In another medium bowl, whisk the eggs. Add the lemon zest, melted butter, and milk. Whisk to combine.
4. Pour the egg mixture over the flour mixture and whisk for about 3 minutes until very smooth.
5. Pour the batter into the prepared pan. Arrange the cherries on top.
6. Bake for 30 minutes or until the clafoutis is set and golden. Let cool for 10 minutes, and dust with the powdered sugar before serving.

4-6
10 minutes
30 minutes

Nutrition: Calories: 188; Fat: 7g; Carbs: 28g; Protein: 4g

Orange And Almond Cake

Ingredients:
- ½ cup olive oil, + more for greasing
- 1 cup ground almonds
- 1½ cups sugar, divided
- 2 tsp baking powder
- 4 large eggs
- Grated zest of 2 oranges
- 1 cup freshly squeezed orange juice
- 5 whole cloves
- Grated zest of 1 lemon
- ¼ tsp ground cardamom

Directions:
1. Preheat the oven to 350°F. Coat an 8-inch round cake pan with olive oil. Set aside.
2. In a medium bowl, stir together the almonds, 1 cup of sugar, and the baking powder.
3. Whisk the eggs, olive oil, and orange zest in another medium bowl. Add the egg mixture to the almond mixture.
4. Whisk well to combine and spoon into the prepared cake pan. Bake on the middle rack for 45 minutes or until the top is golden.
5. Meanwhile, stir the remaining ½ cup of sugar, orange juice, cloves, lemon zest, and cardamom in your medium saucepan over medium heat.
6. Let it boil, stirring occasionally, and cook for 5 to 8 minutes until the mixture is syrupy. Set aside.
7. Remove the cake from the oven. Drizzle it with the syrup and let it soak into the cake. Let the cake rest for 30 minutes before serving.

15 minutes + resting time
45 minutes
8

Nutrition: Calories: 371; Fat: 19g; Carbs: 47g; Protein: 6g

Crème Caramel

Ingredients:
- 1½ cups sugar, divided
- ½ cup water, + more as needed
- 3 cups milk
- 4 large egg yolks
- 2 tsp vanilla extract
- Grated zest of 1 orange

Directions:
1. Preheat the oven to 325°F.
2. In a heavy-bottomed saucepan over low heat, combine 1 cup of sugar and the water.
3. Cook until the sugar dissolves, carefully brushing the pot's walls with a bit of water to prevent the sugar from crystallizing on the sides.
4. Adjust to medium-high heat and boil until a syrup forms and turns golden brown.
5. Remove and carefully pour the syrup into 6 ramekins. Set aside to cool.
6. Heat the milk in your medium saucepan over medium heat until hot but not boiling.
7. In your medium bowl, whisk the egg yolks with the remaining ½ cup of sugar, vanilla, and orange zest.
8. While whisking continuously, slowly add the warmed milk to the egg mixture until well combined.
9. Using a fine-mesh sieve, strain the milk-and-egg mixture into a bowl. Pour the strained mixture into the ramekins.
10. Place the ramekins in your large roasting pan and add enough water to come halfway up the sides of the ramekins.
11. Bake for about 35 minutes or until the custard is just set. Remove from the oven, carefully remove the ramekins from the hot water, and let cool for 15 minutes.
12. Cover and refrigerate for 3 hours before serving. To unmold, run your sharp knife around the inside of each ramekin and carefully invert it onto a serving plate.

2
20 min + chilling time
20 minutes

Nutrition: Calories: 288; Fat: 6g; Carbs: 57g; Protein: 6g

Sweet desserts

Red Wine-Poached Pears

Ingredients:

> 4 cups dry red wine or cranberry juice
> 1 cup sugar
> ½ cup dried cranberries
> Grated zest of 1 lemon
> 4 Bosc pears, peeled with stems intact

Directions:

1. Combine the red wine, sugar, cranberries, and lemon zest in your large saucepan over medium heat. Let it boil.
2. Using tongs, gently lower the pears into the boiling mixture. Adjust to low heat, cover the pan, and simmer for 20 minutes, turning the pears every 5 minutes.
3. Remove the pears and place them on a platter. Set aside.
4. Adjust to low heat and cook the liquid for 5 to 10 minutes more until it is slightly syrupy.
5. Drizzle the liquid over the pears and let the pears cool slightly before serving.
6. Slice the pears in half, if desired, and drizzle with the syrup. Let them cool slightly before serving.

5 minutes

25-30 minutes

4

Nutrition: Calories: 335; Fat: 1g; Carbs: 71g; Protein: 1g

Classic Rice Pudding

Ingredients:

> 4 cups 2% milk
> ¾ cup sugar
> 2 whole cloves
> 2 cinnamon sticks
> 6 cups water
> ½ cup short-grain rice
> 2 large eggs
> ¼ tsp ground cinnamon
> ¼ cup chopped toasted almonds (optional)

Directions:

1. In your heavy-bottomed saucepan over medium heat, stir the milk and sugar together. Next, add the cloves and cinnamon sticks.
2. Cook for 15 minutes until the milk bubbles along the edges but does not boil. Turn off the heat. Let sit for 10 minutes. Set aside.
3. In your medium saucepan over medium heat, combine the water and rice.
4. Cook for 15 minutes until the rice is cooked but not mushy. Drain the rice and add it to the cooked, cooled milk.
5. Return the saucepan with the milk and rice mixture to medium heat. Cook for 30 minutes, often stirring until thickened.
6. Remove and remove and discard the cloves and cinnamon sticks. Set aside.
7. In a small bowl, whisk the eggs until frothy. Whisk in about ½ cup of the milk-and-rice mixture and mix well. Pour this back into the saucepan.
8. Return the saucepan to medium heat. Cook for 5 minutes, stirring constantly.
9. Spoon the pudding into custard cups, dust with the cinnamon, and top with the toasted almonds (if using).

6

10 minutes

1 hour & 20 minutes

Nutrition: Calories: 276; Fat: 7g; Carbs: 46g; Protein: 9g

No-Bake Spiced Fig Loaf

Ingredients:
- 1½ pounds dried Mission figs, stemmed & finely chopped
- 1 cup almonds, toasted and finely chopped
- ½ cup orange marmalade
- ¼ cup granulated sugar
- 1 tbsp olive oil, + more for moistening
- 1 tbsp aniseed
- 1 tsp ground cinnamon
- ¼ tsp ground nutmeg
- Grated zest of 1 orange
- 1 tbsp powdered sugar

Directions:
1. Combine the figs and almonds in a food processor and pulse for 1 minute.
2. Add the marmalade, granulated sugar, olive oil, aniseed, cinnamon, nutmeg, and orange zest. Pulse until well combined.
3. Spoon the mixture into a medium bowl, knead for 10 minutes, and shape into a large loaf.
4. Moisten a large piece of wax paper with a bit of olive oil and wrap the wax paper around the loaf. Refrigerate for 2 days before cutting and serving.
5. Dust with powdered sugar before serving.

20 minutes + chilling time
0 minutes
8

Nutrition: Calories: 264; Fat: 9g; Carbs: 48g; Protein: 4g

Cinnamon Biscotti

Ingredients:
- 2 cups all-purpose flour
- 3 tsp ground cinnamon, divided
- 1 tsp baking powder
- ¼ tsp salt
- 1 cup sugar divided
- 6 tbsp unsalted butter at room temperature
- 3 large eggs
- ¼ cup freshly squeezed orange juice
- 1 tsp vanilla extract

Directions:
1. Preheat the oven to 325°F. Line a baking sheet with parchment paper.
2. Whisk the flour, 2 tsp cinnamon, baking powder, and salt in a medium bowl. Set aside.
3. Combine all but 2 tablespoons of sugar and the butter in a large bowl. Using a handheld electric mixer, beat until fluffy.
4. Add 2 eggs and beat well to combine. Mix in the orange juice and vanilla until blended.
5. Add the flour mixture to your butter mixture and combine until a dough forms. Divide the dough in half.
6. Shape each half into a 9-inch-long log. Transfer the logs to your baking sheet.
7. In your small bowl, whisk the remaining egg. Finally, brush the logs with the egg wash.
8. Bake for 40 minutes. Remove and let cool for 20 minutes. Leave the oven on.
9. In a small bowl, stir together the reserved 2 tablespoons of sugar and the remaining 1 teaspoon of cinnamon.
10. Cut the logs at a 45-degree angle into ½-inch-thick slices using a serrated knife. Place the biscotti, cut side down, on a baking sheet.
11. Dust with the cinnamon sugar and bake for 15 minutes. Let cool for a couple of hours before serving.

30
20 min + cooling time
55 minutes

Nutrition: Calories: 170; Fat: 6g; Carbs: 27g; Protein: 3g

Sweet desserts

Nut Butter Cup Fat Bomb

Ingredients:
- ½ cup crunchy almond butter
- ½ cup light fruity extra-virgin olive oil
- ¼ cup ground flaxseed
- 2 tbsp unsweetened cocoa powder
- 1 tsp vanilla extract
- 1 tsp ground cinnamon (optional)
- 1 to 2 tsp sugar-free sweetener of choice (optional)

Directions:
1. In a mixing bowl, combine the almond butter, olive oil, flaxseed, cocoa powder, vanilla, cinnamon (if using), and sweetener (if using).
2. Pour into 8 mini muffin liners and freeze until solid, at least 12 hours. Store in the freezer to maintain their shape.

5 minutes + freezing time

0 minutes

8

Nutrition: Calories: 240; Fat: 24g; Carbs: 5g; Protein: 3g

Chocolate Chia Pudding

Ingredients:
- 2 cups heavy cream
- ¼ cup unsweetened cocoa powder
- 1 tsp almond extract or vanilla extract
- ½ or 1 tsp ground cinnamon
- ¼ tsp salt
- ½ cup chia seeds

Directions:
1. In a saucepan, heat the heavy cream over medium-low heat to just below a simmer. Remove and allow to cool slightly.
2. Combine the warmed heavy cream, cocoa powder, almond extract, cinnamon, and salt in a blender until the cocoa is well incorporated.
3. Stir in the chia seeds and let sit for 15 minutes.
4. Divide the mixture evenly between ramekins or small glass bowls and refrigerate for at least 6 hours or until set. Serve chilled.

4

10 min + chilling time

0 minutes

Nutrition: Calories: 561; Fat: 53g; Carbs: 19g; Protein: 8g

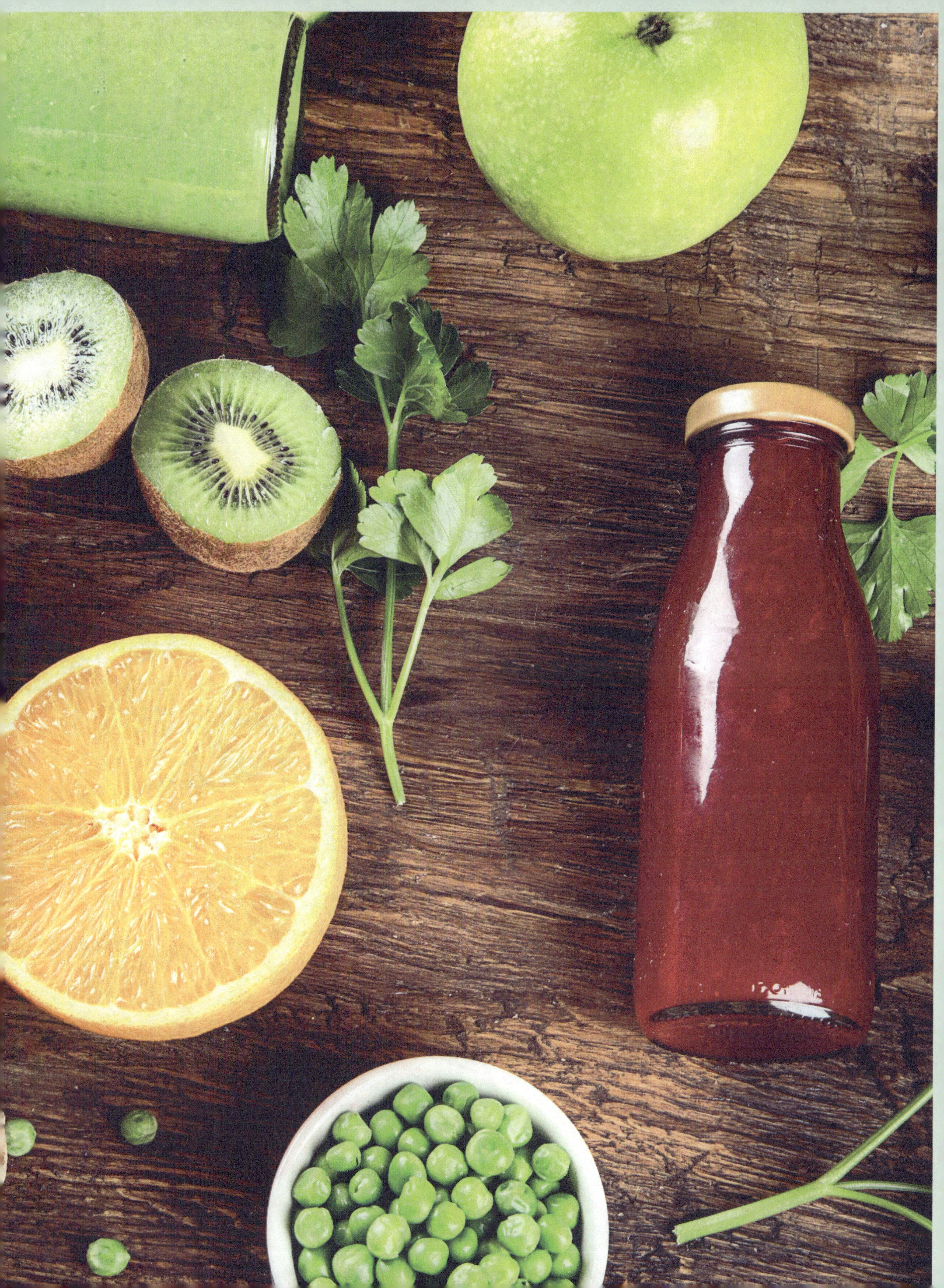

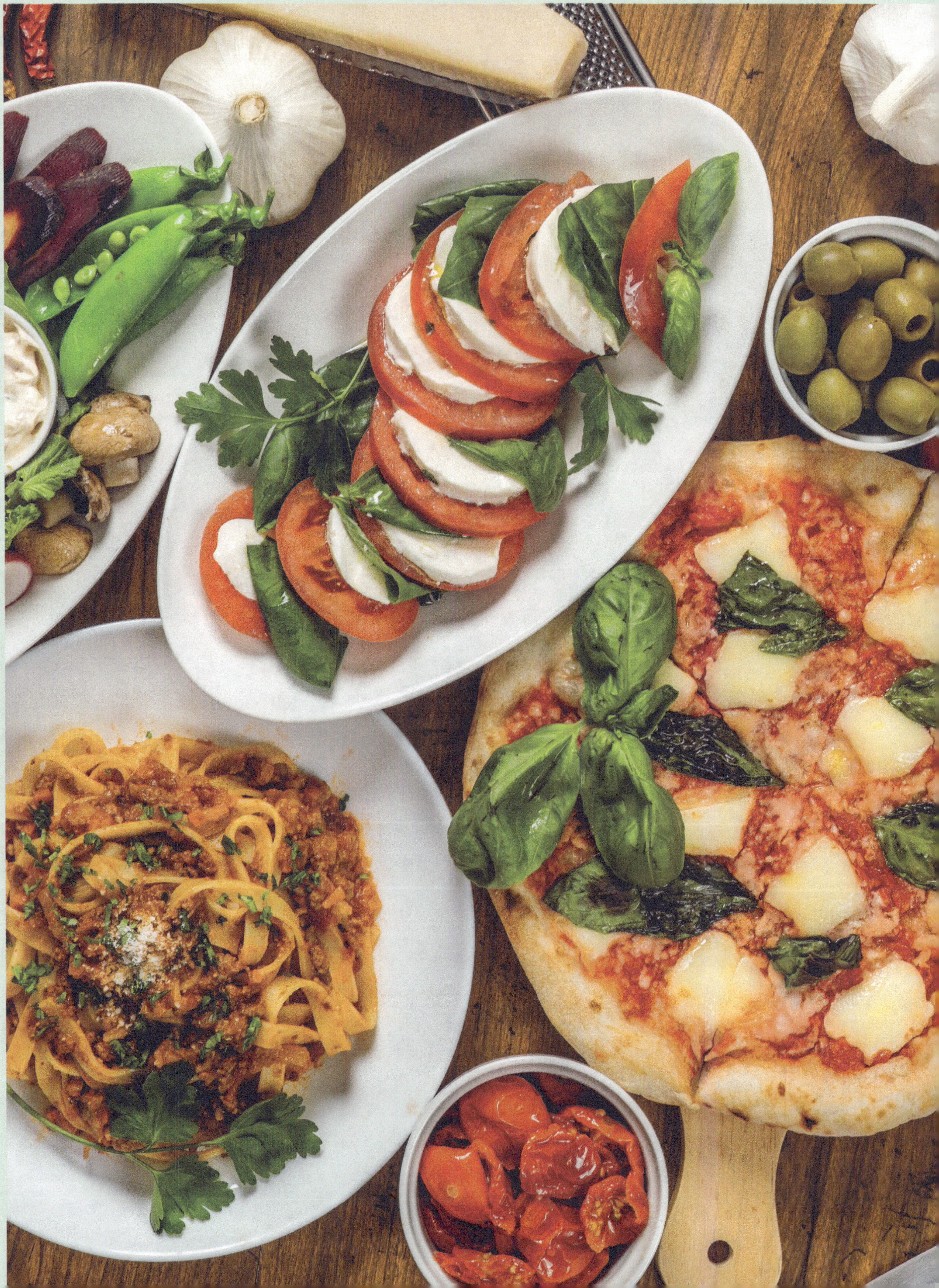

CHAPTER 10

30-day meal plan

DAY	BREAKFAST	LUNCH	DINNER	SNACKS/DESSERTS
1	Greek Egg and Tomato Scramble	Cauliflower Steaks with Olive Citrus Sauce	Garlicky Shrimp with Mushrooms	Citrus-Marinated Olives
2	Orange French Toast	Yogurt-Marinated Chicken Kebabs	Greek Turkey Burger	Strawberry Panna Cotta
3	Almond and Maple Quick Grits	Cauliflower Tabbouleh Salad	Flounder with Tomatoes and Basil	Roasted Za'atar Chickpeas
4	Scrambled Eggs with Goat Cheese	Citrus-Glazed Salmon with Zucchini Noodles	Roasted Eggplant Soup	Chocolate Chia Pudding
5	Honey Nut Granola	Herbed Ricotta–Stuffed Mushrooms	Pan-Fried Pork Chops with Onions	Pistachio-Stuffed Dates
6	Tomato and Zucchini Frittata	Harissa Yogurt Chicken Thighs	French Bean Stew	Nut Butter Cup Fat Bomb

Chapter 10   30-Day meal plan   57

7	Quinoa Breakfast Bowl	Crab Cake Lettuce Cups	Lentil And Mushroom Lasagna	Burrata Caprese Stack
8	Egg Baked in Avocado	Pistachio Mint Pesto Pasta	Greek Stuffed Squid	Cinnamon Biscotti
9	Harissa Shakshuka with Bell Peppers	Swiss Chard and Black-Eyed Pea Pilaf	Moroccan Stuffed Peppers	Marinated Feta and Artichokes
10	Tomato Avocado Toast	Baked Falafel Sliders	Salmon with Tarragon-Dijon Sauce	No-Bake Spiced Fig Loaf
11	Chocolate Banana Smoothie	Crispy Mediterranean Chicken Thighs	Vegetable Paella	Spiced Maple Nuts
12	Fig and Ricotta Toast	Caprese Sandwich	Tuscan Bean Soup with Kale	Clafoutis
13	Fruit Bulgur Breakfast Bowl	Shrimp Ceviche Salad	Burst Cherry Tomato Sauce with Angel Hair Pasta	Manchego Crackers
14	Berry Baked Oatmeal	Chickpeas and Kale with Spicy Pomodoro Sauce	Braised Short Ribs with Red Wine	Classic Rice Pudding
15	Marinara Eggs with Parsley	Orange-Tarragon Chicken Salad Wrap	Ratatouille	Greek Deviled Eggs
16	Greek Yogurt Parfait	Cauliflower Steaks with Olive Citrus Sauce	Garlicky Shrimp with Mushrooms	Red Wine–Poached Pears
17	Pomegranate Cherry Smoothie Bowl	Yogurt-Marinated Chicken Kebabs	Greek Turkey Burger	Smoked Salmon Crudités
18	Asparagus And Swiss Quiche	Cauliflower Tabbouleh Salad	Flounder with Tomatoes and Basil	Orange And Almond Cake

19	Breakfast Polenta	Citrus-Glazed Salmon with Zucchini Noodles	Roasted Eggplant Soup	Cherry Tomato Bruschetta
20	Poached Eggs with Avocado Purée	Herbed Ricotta–Stuffed Mushrooms	Pan-Fried Pork Chops with Onions	Crème Caramel
21	Greek Egg and Tomato Scramble	Harissa Yogurt Chicken Thighs	French Bean Stew	Citrus-Marinated Olives
22	Orange French Toast	Crab Cake Lettuce Cups	Lentil And Mushroom Lasagna	Strawberry Panna Cotta
23	Almond and Maple Quick Grits	Pistachio Mint Pesto Pasta	Greek Stuffed Squid	Roasted Za'atar Chickpeas
24	Scrambled Eggs with Goat Cheese	Swiss Chard and Black-Eyed Pea Pilaf	Moroccan Stuffed Peppers	Chocolate Chia Pudding
25	Honey Nut Granola	Baked Falafel Sliders	Salmon with Tarragon-Dijon Sauce	Pistachio-Stuffed Dates
26	Tomato and Zucchini Frittata	Crispy Mediterranean Chicken Thighs	Vegetable Paella	Nut Butter Cup Fat Bomb
27	Quinoa Breakfast Bowl	Caprese Sandwich	Tuscan Bean Soup with Kale	Burrata Caprese Stack
28	Egg Baked in Avocado	Shrimp Ceviche Salad	Burst Cherry Tomato Sauce with Angel Hair Pasta	Cinnamon Biscotti
29	Harissa Shakshuka with Bell Peppers	Chickpeas and Kale with Spicy Pomodoro Sauce	Braised Short Ribs with Red Wine	Marinated Feta and Artichokes
30	Tomato Avocado Toast	Orange-Tarragon Chicken Salad Wrap	Ratatouille	No-Bake Spiced Fig Loaf

30-Day meal plan

CHAPTER 11

Cooking conversion chart

Volume Equivalents (Dry)

US STANDARD	METRIC (APPROXIMATE)	US STANDARD	METRIC (APPROXIMATE)
⅛ teaspoon	0.5 mL	⅔ cup	156 mL
¼ teaspoon	1 mL	¾ cup	177 mL
½ teaspoon	2 mL	1 cup	235 mL
¾ teaspoon	4 mL	2 cups or 1 pint	475 mL
1 teaspoon	5 mL	3 cups	700 mL
1 tablespoon	15 mL	4 cups or 1 quart	1 L
¼ cup	59 mL	½ gallon	2 L
⅓ cup	79 mL	1 gallon	4 L
½ cup	118 mL		

Volume Equivalents (Liquid)

US STANDARD	US STANDARD (OUNCES)	METRIC (APPROXIMATE)
2 tablespoons	1 fl. oz.	30 mL
¼ cup	2 fl. oz.	60 mL
½ cup	4 fl. oz.	120 mL
1 cup	8 fl. oz.	240 mL
1½ cups	12 fl. oz.	355 mL
2 cups or 1 pint	16 fl. oz.	475 mL
4 cups or 1 quart	32 fl. oz.	1 L
1 gallon	128 fl. oz.	4 L

Weight Equivalents

US STANDARD	METRIC (APPROXIMATE)
½ ounce	15 g
1 ounce	30 g
2 ounces	60 g
4 ounces	115 g
8 ounces	225 g
12 ounces	340 g
16 ounces or 1 pound	455 g

Oven Temperatures

FAHRENHEIT (F)	CELSIUS (C) (APPROXIMATE)
250	120
300	150
325	165
350	180
375	190
400	200
425	220
450	230

Cooking conversion chart

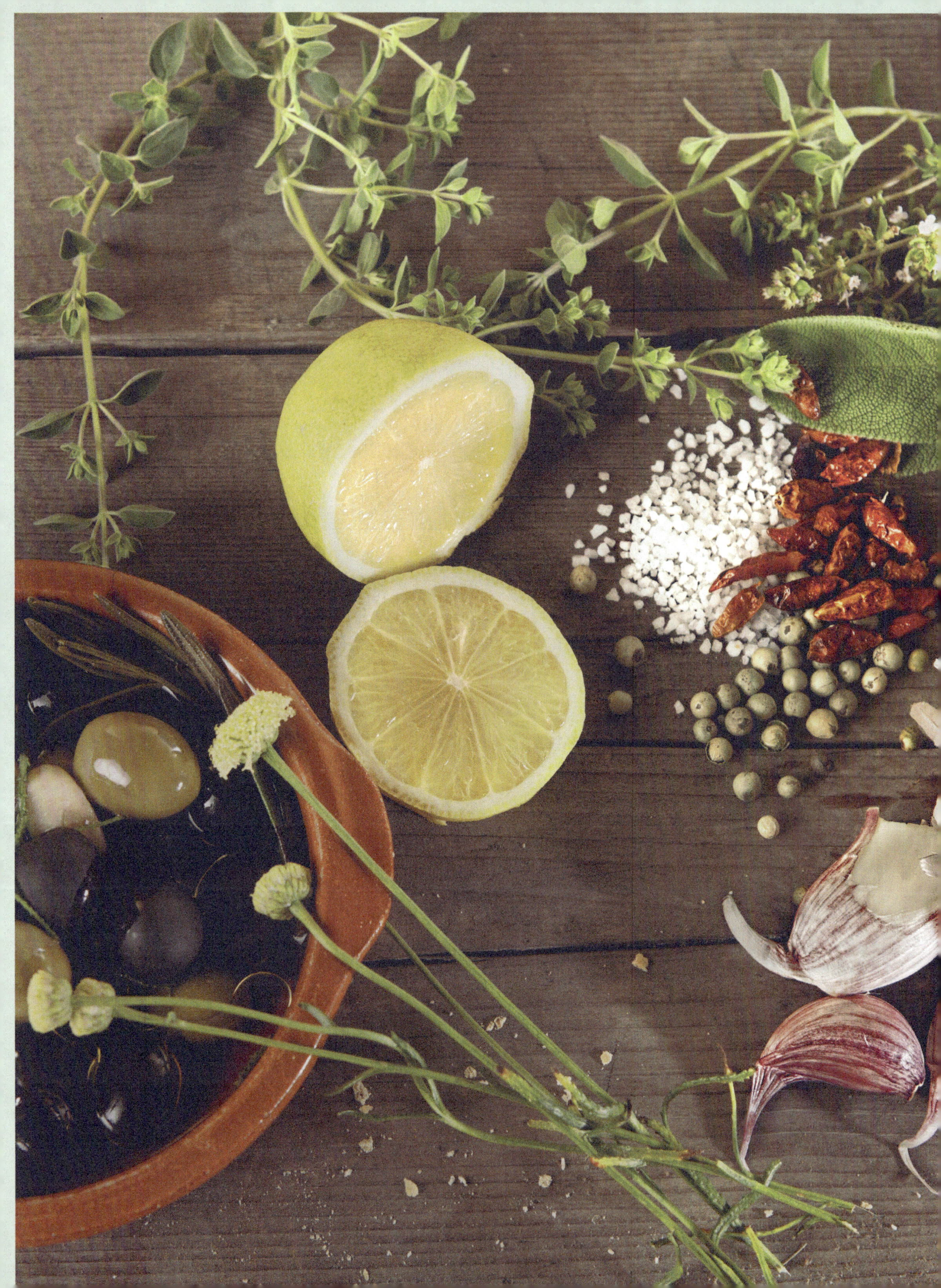

Conclusion

As the Mediterranean diet continues to gain popularity, numerous adaptations and variations have emerged over the years. And for a good reason - it is a versatile style of eating that can be tailored to fit various dietary restrictions and preferences. For example, some may choose to include meat or dairy in moderation in their Mediterranean diet, while others stick to a purely plant-based version. Whatever version one chooses to follow, it is always advised to emphasize fresh, whole foods and to limit the consumption of packaged and processed foods. For instance, incorporating a variety of colorful fruits and vegetables daily ensures a wide range of micronutrients in one's diet, while including healthy fats found in nuts, seeds, and fatty fish provides many health benefits. Additionally, the moderate intake of complex carbohydrates in whole grains is a key source of sustained energy throughout the day. Taking inspiration from the dietary patterns of those living in Mediterranean regions, this balanced and nourishing eating style can impart countless benefits for both long-term health and overall well-being.

Another critical aspect of the Mediterranean diet is the importance of mindful eating and enjoying meals with others. Studies have shown that these practices can significantly benefit physical health and mental well-being. In addition, the Mediterranean diet has been linked to lower rates of depression and other mood disorders and an improved sense of overall life satisfaction. This may be attributed to the healthy fats, lean proteins, and carbohydrates commonly found in this dietary pattern. Beyond the physical and mental health benefits, the Mediterranean lifestyle emphasizes the importance of community, relationships, and slowing down to enjoy life's simple pleasures.

By enjoying leisurely meals with loved ones, engaging in regular physical activity, and finding joy in nature, followers of the Mediterranean diet can experience lower stress levels and a greater sense of purpose and fulfillment in life.

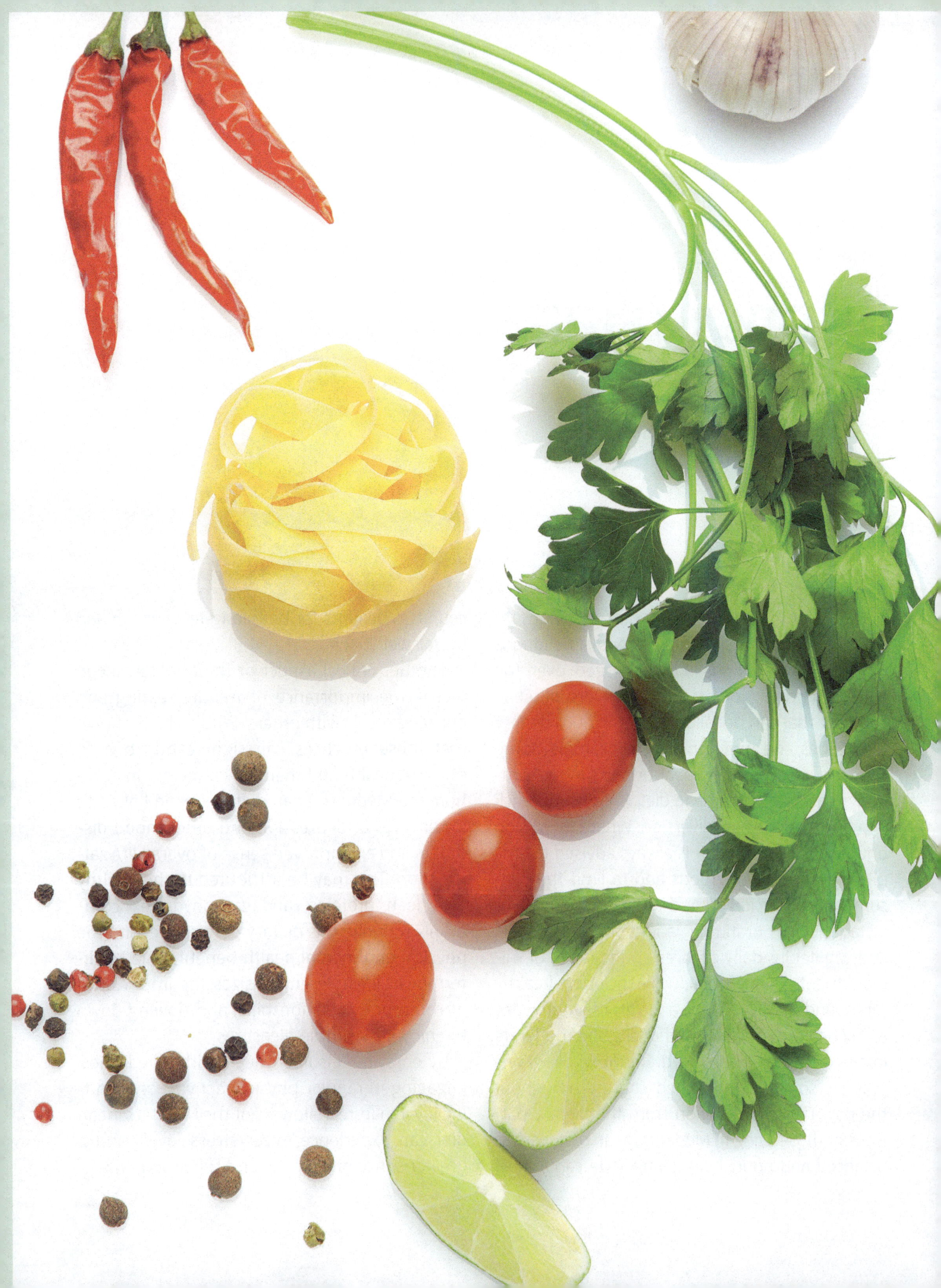

Recipes Index

BREAKFAST RECIPES — 14

Greek Egg and Tomato Scramble — 15
Fig and Ricotta Toast — 15
Poached Eggs with Avocado Purée — 16
Breakfast Polenta — 16
Asparagus And Swiss Quiche — 17
Pomegranate Cherry Smoothie Bowl — 17
Greek Yogurt Parfait — 18
Marinara Eggs with Parsley — 18
Berry Baked Oatmeal — 19
Fruit Bulgur Breakfast Bowl — 19
Chocolate Banana Smoothie — 20
Tomato Avocado Toast — 20
Harissa Shakshuka with Bell Peppers — 21
Egg Baked in Avocado — 21
Quinoa Breakfast Bowl — 22
Tomato and Zucchini Frittata — 22
Honey Nut Granola — 23
Scrambled Eggs with Goat Cheese — 23
Almond and Maple Quick Grits — 24
Orange French Toast — 24

LUNCH RECIPES — 25

Cauliflower Steaks with Olive Citrus Sauce — 26
Baked Falafel Sliders — 26
Orange-Tarragon Chicken Salad Wrap — 27
Chickpeas and Kale with Spicy Pomodoro Sauce — 27
Shrimp Ceviche Salad — 28
Caprese Sandwich — 28
Crispy Mediterranean Chicken Thighs — 29
Swiss Chard and Black-Eyed Pea Pilaf — 29

Recipes index 65

Pistachio Mint Pesto Pasta — 30
Crab Cake Lettuce Cups — 30
Harissa Yogurt Chicken Thighs — 31
Herbed Ricotta–Stuffed Mushrooms — 31
Citrus-Glazed Salmon with Zucchini Noodles — 32
Cauliflower Tabbouleh Salad — 32
Yogurt-Marinated Chicken Kebabs — 33

DINNER RECIPES — 34

Tuscan Bean Soup with Kale — 35
Garlicky Shrimp with Mushrooms — 35
Braised Short Ribs with Red Wine — 36
Ratatouille — 36
Burst Cherry Tomato Sauce with Angel Hair Pasta — 37
Moroccan Stuffed Peppers — 37
Salmon with Tarragon-Dijon Sauce — 38
Vegetable Paella — 38
Lentil And Mushroom Lasagna — 39
Greek Stuffed Squid — 40
French Bean Stew — 40
Pan-Fried Pork Chops with Onions — 41
Roasted Eggplant Soup — 41
Flounder with Tomatoes and Basil — 42
Greek Turkey Burger — 42

SNACK IDEAS — 43

Citrus-Marinated Olives — 44
Manchego Crackers — 44
Cherry Tomato Bruschetta — 45
Smoked Salmon Crudités — 45
Greek Deviled Eggs — 46
Spiced Maple Nuts — 46
Marinated Feta and Artichokes — 47
Burrata Caprese Stack — 47
Pistachio-Stuffed Dates — 48
Roasted Za'atar Chickpeas — 48

SWEET DESSERTS — 49

Strawberry Panna Cotta — 50
Clafoutis — 50
Orange And Almond Cake — 51
Crème Caramel — 51
Red Wine–Poached Pears — 52
Classic Rice Pudding — 52
No-Bake Spiced Fig Loaf — 53
Cinnamon Biscotti — 53
Nut Butter Cup Fat Bomb — 54
Chocolate Chia Pudding — 54

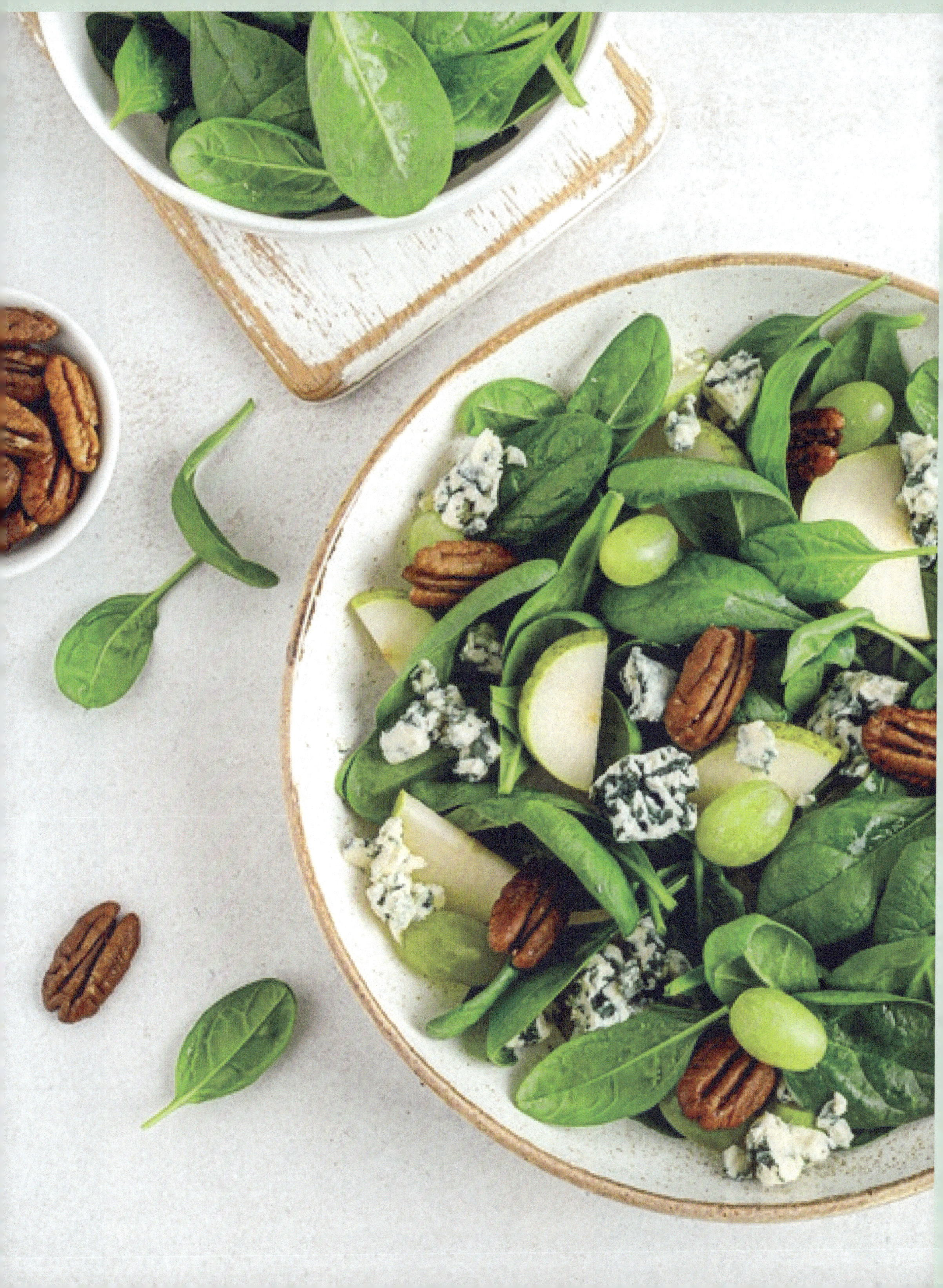

Notes

Notes

Notes

Notes

Notes

Notes

Notes

Notes

Notes

Made in the USA
Coppell, TX
03 May 2023